REVEALING COMPOSITE EFFECT OF SOCIAL MEDIA, NARCISSISM AND SELF IDENTITY

By

PRIYAM SHARMA

CONTENTS

Chapter 1: Introduction	**1-20**
Chapter 2: Review of Literature	**21-32**
Chapter 3: Method	**33-38**
Chapter 4: Results	**39-61**
Chapter 5: Discussion	**62-71**
Chapter 6: Summary and Conclusion	**72-78**
References	**79-90**
Appendices	**91-107**

Chapter I
Introduction

CHAPTER-I
INTRODUCTION

"I fear the day when technology will suppress human interaction and the world will have a generation of idiots"

- Albert Einstein (1879-1955)

The above quote significantly talks about the impending and inevitable consequences of technology in our life. We all are living in an age of unprecedented technological development that is changing the contours of time and space; developments that configure everyone's life and work-life beyond imagination. The developments have created comforts and help amplify our capabilities to transform our notion of who we are and how our experiences are organized. The ideology of modernity with its assumptions of individualism and materialism has nurtured a view of human beings which establishes the physical self as the ultimate reality and consumerism as the pathway. This leads to various lifestyle diseases like diabetes, obesity, stress, anxiety, hypertension, depression, and so on.

Developing countries like India where social media is taken as an important tool for nation-building and people's welfare. It has been considered that the 21st Century is the age of information, communication, and knowledge, and this is the only way the people of the country can be empowered. Today, social media is becoming the most important tool for Nation Building and People's Welfare as the Government is implementing lots of initiatives and schemes for citizen's welfare under social media, for example - digital India, smart city mission, and many more. No one can deny the pervasive presence of social media in today's world. Presently the situation of social media is like a two-edged sword. It may be a boon or it may be a bane. But it depends on how we use it. Therefore we can say that social media itself is like an innocent guy trapped in the conflict of interests of various stakeholders. Some use it in an altruistic way and some use it in a selfish way.

After the increased acceptance of the welfare state, the standard of life of the masses has emerged as the most popular tool to measure the development and achievement of society. The idea is much similar to the concept of ―human development" articulated by the UNDP (United Nations Development Program). In recent times, the world has started accepting the role of people's attitudinal and behavioral dimensions too, in the gamut of development promotion. Human development increases the social welfare and wellbeing of the people and has been the ultimate objective of development planning in India. India, a heterogeneous society where society is full of diversities like different classes, castes, regional differences, religious communities, and split between rural and urban living. These different living styles shape the personality development of Indian people, and in such cases, any disorder can bring huge unconformity in the individual and society at large, which as a consequence can work against the social welfare and wellbeing of people. Focusing on a specific personality disorder is a narcissistic personality disorder which is one of the related other personal and societal disorders.

Over the last few decades, the whole idea about human development has been shifted towards ‗happiness' and ‗life satisfaction' of the citizens. Ryan and Deci (2001) offer a definition for happiness into views: happiness as being hedonic, accompanied with enjoyable feelings and desirable judgments, and happiness as being eudaimonic, which involves doing virtuous, moral, and meaningful things. In 2011 the United Nations General Assembly adopted wellbeing and happiness. The word ‗happiness' is quite complex and should not be used lightly. Happiness is an aspiration of every human being, and can also be a measure of social progress. Yet different countries define happiness differently. Despite all, the key to proper measurement, in WHR 2013 (World Happiness Report) report says that happiness is used in at least two following ways- (the happiness curriculum)

1) As an emotion [‗Were you happy yesterday?']

2) As an evaluation [‗Are you happy with your life as a whole?']

Focusing on evaluation, happiness gives a direction towards life satisfaction. In the sense of life satisfaction, evaluation of self or self-assessment is a better tool. It is a process of introspection which later will give an idea about the self and one's own identity. Individuals, by evaluating themselves can develop a sense of self and life satisfaction. Self-evaluation is another term for self-assessment, which is the process of looking at oneself in order to assess aspects that are important to one's identity. So far as self-identity is concerned, it is the perception or recognition of one's characteristics as a particular individual, especially in relation to social context.

Self and Identity are the terms that are used sometimes interchangeably. and sometimes connoting different aspects of human existential reality. In order to find the theoretical relationship between self and identity, some important views by different scholars are given below–

William James, an American philosopher, and psychologist described the perception of self

1) The self is composed of our thoughts and beliefs about ourselves or in the terms of James ―known" or more simplified manner is about "ME".
2) The self is also the active processor of information. In James's terms ―knower" or more simplified manner is about ―I'.

But in modern terms, psychologists refer to the ―known" as the self-concept and ―knower" as awareness or consciousness.

Paranjpe (1998) identify three important meaning of Identity

1) The quality or condition of being the same in substance, composition, nature, properties, or in particular qualities under consideration, absolute or essential sameness or oneness. (Philosophical implications of identity.)
2) The condition or fact that a person or a thing is itself and not something else. (At the heart of the forensic conception of personhood.)
3) The condition of being identified in feeling, interest, and the like. (The implication when someone speaks of one's ‗Indian Identity' or my identity as a social activist.)

Identity is related to social and observable (outer) and self is related to personal and experiential (inner).

1.1. Social Media

In the recent past, it has become so influential that it started interfering in the lives of individuals. Social media has penetrated the lives of every common man, with the advancement of technology and advent of smart-phones, high-speed internet facilities at lower rates, and user-friendly applications and the list is long. The main aim of social media was to provide a platform to introduce a space for people to interact with their loved ones, the ones who are not easily accessible, to share important information, to express their ideas and suggestions, and to update events. But gradually became one where asocial and introverts started finding virtual friends with whom they can interact freely. Social media has become a platform for people to satisfy their own need for acceptance, recognition, and ventilation. People with passive personality traits try to learn to use social media platform purposefully to express their productive, creative ideas and opinions related to various issues which they find difficult to do in their real life, and on the other hand, there are some other people for the social media become a place for expressing their aggressive motives and involving in virtual aggression which may be physical, emotional, sexual or social.

Social media are not mere sites where one can meet other people and exchange with them or upload pictures. The definition of social media is not absolute, nor it claims that it contains firm boundaries. In today's world, the media is connected to almost everything that humans interact with. Social media contains different sites like tinder, youtube, weblogs, Whatsapp, Facebook, Instagram, Twitter, online magazines, internet forums, video sharing communities, and so forth (L Hur, J., & Gupta, M. 2013) and these are the current tools of teenager communication now as days. Social media is becoming a space where people are living virtual lives. People who access social media consistently have started living in a virtual world rather than living a life of their own. This gives rise to the issue of fantasy versus reality where they generally fail to distinguish between the virtual and the real world. (fantasy Vs. Reality) But in some cases, people deliberately decrease their time in real life and feel happy and satisfied in virtual life. They believe that it is a cure to alleviate their distress. But in a real scenario, one who approaches this stage we can infer that they are actually in the process of getting addicted to social media.

In the era of globalization, swift technological advances have had significant bearings on our understanding of the social world. Satellite television (TV), Internet services, and other services are expanding at an unbelievable pace, creating both excitement and confusion in the minds of the youth and children. These hovering and intruding technologies have changed the notion of the family. In order to identify the impact of TV and television advertising on children, Unnikrishnan and Bajpai (1996) showed how the dominant images being created by TV serials, cartoons, and commercials could have disastrous effects on these vulnerable and impressionable minds at a tender age. nowadays children are developing their understanding of the social world, largely by watching TV. Media people are continuously working in order to make these platforms attractive and their major concern is to sell dreams and a vision of society which is in sharp contrast to the experiences of real-life settings, which further creates conflicts in the mind of the youth as well as children. A noteworthy issue in the context of the effect of media is violence on children and the youth. Various researches strongly suggested that observation of violence in the mass media not only stimulates aggressive behavior in the short run by priming aggressive scripts and schemes, but also stimulates aggressive behavior in the long run by changing schemes, scripts, and beliefs about aggression' (Anderson and Huesmann,2003:309). In the arena of increasing violence in society, one needs to understand what norms are formed and reinforced via the excessive depiction of violence in the media.

Conversely, the media also play a positive role in order to promote social cohesiveness, disease prevention, and development.

1.2. Social Media Addiction

Since, last decades the health and wellbeing has become a key issue of the contemporary developing society and attracted a greater amount of research (Dalal & Mishra, 2006; Nadidoo & wills, 2000; Keyes & Grzywacz, 2005; Keyes, 2002.2003a. 2003b). The word health originated from the old English word ‒health" which means a state of bier and was generally used to infer a ‒soundness of the body"(Dolfman, 1973). According to Nadidoo & Wills (2000), health can refer to mean the absence of disease or desirability also at the same time refers to a state of fitness and ability or to a reservoir of personal resources that can be called when needed (Nadidoo & Wills, 2000). People with different socio-cultural backgrounds may hold different conceptions of health and an individual may have different ideas about the meaning of health depending upon the circumstances under which the issue is raised.

Definition of Addiction can be defined as an individual who can't quit taking specific medication or concoction has a substance reliance. A few addictions additionally include a failure to quit participating in exercises, for example, betting, eating, or working. In these conditions, an individual has a social fixation. In 1964 a WHO Expert Committee presented the term ‗dependence' to supplant the terms ‗addiction' and ‗habituation' The term can be utilized by and large concerning the entire scope of psychoactive drugs (drug dependence, chemical dependence, substance use dependence), or with specific reference to a particular drug or class of drugs (e.g. alcohol dependence, opioid dependence).

Currently, technologies like - mobile, tablets, and the internet are frequently used by people to meet day to day needs. Technologies have made our living easier and now, one cannot imagine life without technologies. Mobile phones and the internet help in facilitating communication among people. Social networking through mobile phones and the internet are common in today's world, the young population being the most commonly affected ones. Adolescents use different types of gadgets like cell phones, tablets, laptops, I-pads, etc. Some use it for just mere communication. Some use it for entertainment (watching movies, listening to music, playing online games), shopping, browsing educational materials, etc., other than communication. The use of technology is essential to make the tasks of life easier; however it's abnormal, excessive, unnecessary use leads to addiction and makes life more difficult. Though there is no standard definition for ―Technology addiction", the attempt of Shaw & Black (2008) to define ―Internet addiction" as – ―an excessive or poorly controlled preoccupation, urges or behaviors related to use of internet and computers, that is significantly impairing and distressing" also valid for any other technologies like – mobile or pager, etc. Another way of defining technology 171 addiction is – a habitual and compulsive way of indulgence with technology deviating from meeting life's different issues. So internet addiction or a person is called to be addicted when he/she is unable to control the urge to check social media and feels a lacuna when deprived of accessing the internet. It also interferes with the well being of an individual by giving a feeling of distress and restlessness. It also gives rise to attention seeking attitude when someone does not give an instant reply.

In defining social media addiction, most vulnerable people are the one who feels lonely, the one who feels that they are not being properly understood by people around them, the one who believes that they are a victim of reality and wants to escape from it, the one who lacks opportunities or have difficulty in expressing their thoughts and emotions, the one who is guided by the need for recognition and the one who feel that they have been under consistent social control and suppression. In this stage people start experiencing withdrawal symptoms including emotional outbursts, isolating themselves and they even experience moderate to severe depression when they are restricted from using social media. They develop the idea that whatever happens in the social media is real. (they don't want to accept the reality) Addicted people find it hard to differentiate between real life happenings and their experiences in social media and start showing behavioral symptoms like low decision making process, low productivity, exhibiting state of confusion, high level of disturbances in working memory, deterioration in long-term memory, frequent slip into a delirious state, even they take excessive time to complete a simple task.

1.3. Narcissism

The term narcissism comes from the mythical Greek character Narcissus, who fell in love with himself after he saw his own image reflected in the water. It is when an individual develops exaggerated feelings of self-importance, self-loving, and excessively high self-esteem. Besides, in combination with these, it is a personality trait that is characterized by low empathy towards others. Sigmund Freud in his essay on narcissism explains the term as the "Love of the self" in the libidinal drive. According to him, a narcissist is a person who is in love with himself who obtains his / her sexual satisfaction from admiring himself/herself in the mirror and care his/her body. Theoretically, narcissism is defined by the Diagnostic and Statistical Manual of

Mental Disorder IVth edition; American Psychiatric Association (1994) Define as a pervasive pattern of grandiosity, self importance, and self focus; DSM- IV, define, narcissism person is preoccupied with dreams of success, power, beauty, and brilliance. Generally, there are two types of narcissism - Grandiose and Vulnerable narcissism. It is increasingly recognized that there are at least two forms of narcissism, which might be most aptly titled ―grandiose narcissism" and ―vulnerable narcissism" (e.g., Dickinson & Pincus, 2003; Fossati et al., 2005; Miller & Campbell, 2008; Miller et al., 2011; Russ, Shedler, Bradley, & Westen, 2008; Wink, 1991; Wright, Lukowitsky, Pincus, &Conroy, 2010). Grandiosity is characterized by dominance, aggression, self-assurance, arrogant attitudes, inflated self-esteem, exploitativeness, entitlement, and a strong need for the admiration of others. Vulnerability, in contrast, is characterized by fragile self-esteem, emotional instability, introversion, negative affect, hostility, need for recognition, entitlement, egocentricity, and preoccupation with grandiose fantasies, an oscillation between feelings of superiority and inferiority (Hendin & Cheek, 1997; Miller et al., 2011).

Significantly narcissism syndrome is highly complex to define and measure. It is a highly distinctive dynamic system of a social, cognitive, and affective dynamic system of social, cognitive and affective self regulatory process (Carolyn C. Morf& Frederic Rhodewalt, 2001)

An obsession that today's teens are having with sharing their different phases of lives on social media has led them to believe that this group is growing up to be narcissists. Narcissism (or narcissistic personality disorder NPD) is a mental disorder in which people have an inflated sense of their own importance, a deep need for admiration and a lack of empathy for others." While nowadays young adults go through a "narcissistic" period in their lives to establish their own identity and break away from caregivers. Some of the negative traits associated with narcissism suggest that social media sites are promoting earlier adoption of narcissistic behavior.

1.4. Self Identity

The two concepts of 'self' and 'identity' implicate each other. In the modern era, entire inquiries are concerned with human affairs positively which implicate the idea of self. According to James (1890), a person's self is the "sum total of all that he calls his." He was the first person who suggests that people have many "selves", such as real self, ideal self, and social self. Jersild (1965) emphasizes on concept of self, that the self, as it finally evolves, is made up of all that goes into a person's experiences of his individual existence. It is a person's "inner world." It is a composite of a person's thoughts and feelings, strivings and hopes, fear and fantasies, his view of what he is, what he has been, what he might become, and his attitudes pertaining to his worth. Allport (1961) describes self in this way, that the self is something of which we are immediately aware. We think of it as the warm, central, private region of our life. As such it plays a crucial part in our consciousness (a concept broader than self), in our personality (a concept broader than consciousness), and in our organism (a concept broader than personality). Thus it is some kind of core in our being. (Hurlock 1988).

Understanding of self offers a foundation for one's experience of being in the world and a tool for a person or group to coordinate joint action and move towards cherished goals.

Self is a person's essential being that distinguishes them from others, especially considered as the object of introspection or reflexive action. It is defined as the individual person who seems like an object of his or her own reflective consciousness. The idea of self in the Indian context which defines self / true self as deeper and having inner consciousness which identifies that individual with the entire universe or cosmos. It recognizes a single unity in life and all entities are supposed to share common attributes.

Identity construction is a continuous process that develops through successive stages over the course of socialization with intra-psychic and relational roots (Scabini & Cigoli, 2000). People can identify with lots of different groups, like their gender, race, nationality, or politics. Self identity is defined as having clearly self defined goals, values, and beliefs, on which a person is unequivocally committed. Which helps give direction, purpose, and meaning to life. Social media impacts on the construction and reconstruction of self identity of an individual which may be destined to create differences from his/her social identity. Identity formation is influenced by relationships with family, educators, and peers (Culbertson et all.,2003) but the extent of the impact of social media use on crucial aspects of development is not yet clear.

Adams and Marshall (1996) identify the concept of identity and proposed five important roles of identity that include the following:

1) Identity aids in providing a basis and structure for comprehending and knowing oneself.

2) It presents a means of both personal control and free will.

3) Through values, commitments, and goals, it presents a sense of meaning and direction.

4) It aims toward consistency, unity, and harmony between values, beliefs, and commitments.

5) It facilitates the acknowledgment of potential through a sense of future, opportunities, and various choices.

With the help of different and several researches, Adams & Marshall believe in the selfhood in the identity i.e. –

1) Identity is proposed to be a social-psychological construct. In this view, the formation of what is vital to the self and to others is represented by the social influences by means of imitation and identification processes and dynamic self-constructions.

2) The active self-constructive aspects of identity are based upon cognitive or ego operations. These operations are believed to arrange, structure and create/recreate information about the self.

3) When viewed as a psychological structure, identity is a self-regulatory system that functions to focus attention, manage impressions, filter or process information and select suitable behaviours.

4) Identity, as a construct, contains its own useful purpose similar to all social-psychological constructs

Self-identity comprises a number of "self-images" that lie on a continuum, with personalized self-schemata at one extreme and self-characteristics related to social categories at the other (Hagger, Anderson, Kyriakaki, Darkings, 2007).

Cheek (1989) defined PI as private self-conceptions and subjective feelings, and SI as public image and social roles and relationships. personal or individual self, which reflects our private beliefs about our psychological traits and abilities; relational self, which reflects how we see

ourselves in the context of our intimate relationships; social self, which reflects how we see ourselves in more general interpersonal contexts, including our social roles and reputation (i.e., self-presentation); collective self, which reflects how we represent our various reference group identities.

1) Personal identity orientation - Personal or individual self, which reflects our private beliefs about our psychological traits and abilities. It is a private conception of self and feelings of continuity and uniqueness or personal identity. Cheek (1989) defines Personal Identity as private-conceptions and subjective feelings. Cheek and Busch (1982) found Personal Identity was positively correlated with private self consciousness, the need for uniqueness and achievement-oriented self. Individual self reflects a person which is a subjective uniqueness. Such Individual self comprises characteristics such as their traits and behavior, hobbies and interests, aspirations and goals, which helps individuals to differentiate the person from others.

2) Relational identity orientation – Relational self, in general, base identity is related to close relationships furthermore, you truly need to impart your actual self to somebody else. We strive to make progress toward bona fide closeness, to comprehend the contemplations and dreams of your accomplice or dear companion. This view of relationship asserts the power of the relational self. People show a foremost want for

the development of stable relational connections, upgrade and ensure their connections, oppose the end of existing connections, and feel mental and physical torment when socially rejected (Baumeister and Leary 1995; Eisenberger et al. 2003; Murray et al. 1996). In addition, close relationships show their

3) Social identity orientation – Social self, which reflects how we see ourselves in more general interpersonal contexts including our social roles and reputation. It is about social roles and relationships. Cheek (1989) defines Social Identity as a public image and social roles and relationships. Cheek and Busch (1982) found Social Identity to be positively correlated with public self consciousness, sociability and institutional and altruistic selves. Cross cultural research on social identity by Dhawan, Roseman, Naidu, Thapa, and Rettek(1995) found that Indian participants made a large number of references in respect to social identities. They describe themselves using terms like role, group, caste, class, and gender. Just opposite to American people who give their response towards self identity. This concludes that in India, individualism is subordinated to Familialism and it makes sense that self in India is less individual

4) Collective identity orientation - which reflects how we represent our various reference group identities. Cheek(1989) defines Collective Identity as a member in and identification with different groups and collectives such as religious, national, or ethnic groups. Focusing on the study of cross cultural relationships Asian Americans were found significantly higher in CI than European-Americans (Cheek, Tropp, and Chen, 1994). A country like India whose culture has a collectivist identity and prescribes a group orientation(Jones,1990). It has been said that people from collectivist countries are found to emphasize the familial and

social aspect of self concept (Watkins et al., 1998). In the context of India, a collectivistically oriented self construal has been posited. In the study of J.B.P.Sinha, T.N.Sinha, Jyoti Verma, and R.B.N.Sinha (2001) tries to analyse the choice of collectivist or individualist behavior and intentions in the multi-ethnic study. However, they found that concerns for family or family members evoked purely collectivist behavior.

5) Superficial identity orientation - which refers to a measure of an emphasis on surface qualities of self immediately visible to others. Additional use of an ad hoc "scale" of SP items. Superficial Identity scale from the AIQ item pool, and Dollinger (1996) made a 3-item ad hoc scale for Academic/College Identity and they have also made some analyses involving individual AIQ items. Theoretical explanations of superficial identity make believe about superficial relationships, relationships that lack depth which leads to experience feeling of loneliness. In the study done by Wheeless, Zakahi, and Chan (1988) found that the effects of loneliness and self-disclosure based on perceptions and masculine and feminine cues.

People scoring high on narcissism have difficulty maintaining healthy, long-term close relationships and have a tendency to behave aggressively in response to critical feedback. In extreme cases, narcissism can be a clinical disorder affecting the mental health, physical health and well-being of an individual. Narcissistic people have a number of difficulties in maintaining healthy and strong interpersonal relationships. Social relationships are fundamental to fulfilling core human needs, such as the need to belong. They are also implicated in psychological well-being, mental health, and physical health – more socially connected people are more mentally and physically robust and even live longer than less socially connected people. Nowadays, people are increasingly getting connected to social networking websites like Facebook, Twitter, Whatsapp and Instagram, where users themselves publish content publicly in contrast to the traditional mass media(TV, Radio, etc.) that are being relayed by the government or corporate controlled entities. We all know that social media directly or indirectly affects how people establish more values, pursue specific interests, and hobbies, and develop a cohesive self, and excessive engagement with these social media may create the symptoms of self-obsession, self-centric attitude and low empathy toward others. This is mainly attributed to the relative isolation from society because of spending a bigger time on this virtual media and simultaneously ignoring or avoiding the social interactions on the ground.

1.5. Rationale of the Study

1.5.1. Study Relevant to Society

The different aspects of my study enable it to analyse with several dimensions of socio-psychological realities regarding the impact of social media on the creation and recreation of self-identity in youth, because of exposure to a variety of content on social media, along with the critical analysis of how the excessive use of social media could lead to the formation of narcissistic-self characteristics among adults.

In many circumstances, the illicit and provoking contents on social media have resulted into incidents like- riots (Muzaffarnagar, UP), rumors (mass exodus of North-Eastern people from southern India in 2012), mob lynching in Assam, Uttar Pradesh, Rajasthan, different societal and caste conflicts in several parts of the country. Besides, the exposure of youth with the diverse categories of content on social media is constructing, reconstructing their image and identities regarding themselves and leads to the formation of new self-identity which might not be based on constitutional values and principles likes equality, justice, secularism and particularly fraternity/brotherhood, rather, their self-identity may form on the basis of hatred, self-vested interested ignoring mutual respect and understanding, or may be formed because of anti-national sentiments, separatist tendencies or insurgencies. All these identities, if a youth imbibes within his/ her SELF, leads to conflicts between constitutional values and self imbibed values and consequently pose threat to the social fabric of India or even to the security and integrity of the nation itself

In such a situation there is a need for academic discourse on the formulation of policies and programs relating to psychological health implications and distortion of self image and perception of youth with regard to social phenomena. This study would certainly provide such kinds of dimensions as far as the social implication is concerned.

1.5.2. Expected Policy Implication of the Study

This study is planned to deal with the creation and recreation of self identity because of getting exposure through diverse kinds of social media content and therefore helpful in formulating National policy regarding psychological health, mood disorder and tensions among different social groups. Also, it is useful in formulating a comprehensive National Policy on Social Media particularly with reference to preventing the radicalization of youth so that the unity and integrity of our nation can be upheld.

The ever-increasing integration and inter-linkages of goods, services, capital, labor, knowledge, ideas, innovation and technologies in the global community today have posed challenges as well as opportunities at almost all fronts making the youth vulnerable and prone to the formation and deformation of self-identity influenced by parochial characteristics(religion, race, ethnicity, caste etc.) as well as new emerging identities, say, for example, the radicalization of youth in the state of Kerala because of coming into contact with ISIS, Islamic terrorist organisation, on social media

Therefore, whatever the big policy document of the national or state government is being prepared today must also consider the expert opinion on how social media and the internet is influencing the mind and personality of Indian youth and how these innovative fastest and cost effective mass media can be utilized in fulfillment of the government welfare, security and economic policies, for example, *National Security Policy, National Cyber Security Policy, National Education Policy, National Policy for Children, National Policy for Women, National Health Policy(Rural and Urban), and National Mental Health Policy, India.*

My research paper and its possible outcome would thus provide the information, results, and interpretation which could be helpful in policy formulation, creating guidelines, rules, regulations and laws as far as formulation National policy for Social Media is concerned. Looking at the rapidly spreading use of social media, we need a National Policy on Social Media, which is yet to be in the initial stage and requires critical approach in a comprehensive manner. The present trend of the problem of mis-utilisation and under or over- utilization of social media by an individual and its subsequent formation of self–identity and narcissism can be changed for utilization in favour of our demographic dividend. Thus, our nation would have a robust, cheaper, safe and optimal use of social media (i.e. core subject of my research paper if utilized properly) it would be an instrument of successful formulation and implementation of government policies and programs associated with regulation or utilization of social media and associated problems.

1.6. Objective

1. To understand the nature and patterns of usage of social media among youth
2. To investigate the impact of social media usage on self identity and narcissism
3. To find out correlation patterns between usage of social media, narcissism and self identity
4. To examine the difference between male and female participants on the usage of social media, self identity and narcissism

1.7. Hypothesis

1. Higher Social media users would show positive relationships with narcissism.
2. Excessive use of social media would create dissociated self identity.
3. There would be significant differences between male and female in the context of social media interaction.
4. Women, in comparison to men, would score high on the social media addiction scale.
5. Male would show higher narcissistic tendencies in contrast to female.

Chapter II
Review of Literature

CHAPTER-II
REVIEW OF LITERATURES

Mehraj, Bhat and Mehraj (2014) in his journal they describe the various types of impact of the media over individual, family and society as whole. They talk about all the positive and negative impacts of media with describing different theories like the cultivation theories, social learning theories so forth. Media plays both constructive and destructive roles. They concluded their journal by putting the point that people need to decide the limits of their use.

W. Akram, R.Kumar (2017) studied on positive and negative effects of social media in which they focuses on both the side of social media under which they highlight the issues like transforming behaviour styles, use of technologies, including the topic of cyber bullying and others particularly on the field on health, business, education, society and youth.

According to Jane L. Hur and Mayank Gupta (2013) describe how children and adolescents are growing up in the world of web of social networking. Their studies revealed that the impacts are coming out in the form of depression, anxiety, substance abuse and personality disorder out of which the effects are coming on friendship, identity, cognitive growth, and health. However, their studies at the end suggests that, might be social media can be useful at one point, for public health, education, and in fostering creativity.

Danielle Bringham (2010) his thesis tries to explain that whether watching or listening media is going to have some effect or not? This question is deal under the area of violence, alcohol, sex and body image. He found proof that media influence people which changes person's attitude about sex, morals, body image, drinking and reality. Under his research he concluded that on a large scale most student did not believe that their values, norms are influenced by the television and movies.

Bradley M. Waite, Laura E. Levine and Laura L. Bowman (2009) In their study they try to establish a relationship between college student's media use and academic distractibility, impulsiveness, and mental restlessness. Their studies show that in student's instant messaging and reading distracts their academic studies and generates impulsiveness. This study partially supports that there is relation with internal distractibility, a dimension of mental restlessness. This kind of result is same as study done by Levin et al. (2007) where they found in their result that those who use instant messaging and multitasking behavior (doing different work at the same time span) are related to more distractibility for academic reading, had higher motor impulsiveness and lower in attention.

On the other dice of board Tarek A. El-Badawy & Yasmin Hashem (2015) his finding demonstrated that there is no significant relationship between social media and academic performance of school students. He concludes that although students spend hours on social media then to they are much smart enough to manage their time for study and achieve good grades.

Soledad Liliana Escobar-Chaves, Craig A. Anderson (2008) they examine their research among American youth under which they identify that youth are spending their humorous amount of time on using electronic media due to which Centers for

Disease Control and Prevention identify health risk behavior such as obesity, smoking, drinking, sexual risk taking and violence.

In the article of Anna Kende, Adrienn Ujhely, Adam Joinson and Tobias Greitemeyer (2015) mentioned that in modern time we cannot ignore the influence of technology on human being. In today's life our true selves are shown better online added by Bargh, McKenna, & Fitzsimons, 2002. Their study focuses on the relation between social psychological concepts, theories, and methods in social media related studies.

A study done by Madison Ganda (2014) identifies a relationship between identity development within online and offline social networking sites. In which they identify that there is no significant relationship.

The article by Anna Kende, Adrienn Ujhelyi, Adam Joinson and Tobias Greitemeyer (2015) reflects that social media has become the largest platform in which people interact and engage with each other. They focuses on some of the core issues like about self presentation. They added that internet provides unique platform for the enactment of group identity, they also show the social reality of social world, which is affected by internet. They highlighted some issues like internet addiction, loneliness, aggression, online therapies, etc., and other discipline like intra-, inter-personal, social, societal, and cultural level of analysis. Social media has become a powerful tool of cultural globalization which is influenced by its own technological possibilities.

Savci.M and Aysan. F (2017) study on 201 adolescents reveals that effect of four technological addictions such as internet addiction, social media addiction, digital game addiction and smart phone addiction they shows that via these 25% of social connectedness takes place within society negatively and significantly. There is only a prediction about in front of internet. It is making human being away from true social environment, lacking interpersonal relationship.

Brailovskaia J, Margraf J (2017) a longitudinal study investigate that Facebook Addiction Disorder(FAD) is directly and positively related to narcissism personality disorder, toward mental health variables such as depression, anxiety and stress symptoms and physical health. This study results shows that people who intensively use social network sites are at the risk of developing FAD such as facebook related anxiety, but at some point not directly related to physical health. This study at some extent indicates that social media is best platform for narcissistic person, they plan to present themselves to impress a large number of people they are connected with in order of that they spend more time in thinking about and gradually develop vulnerable to FAD

Vivek Agarwal (2015) define technology addiction in adolescence by focusing that they are using technology beyond the control which are causing harm into their behavior such as, abnormally excessive use of technology, rather doing any valued work they are preoccupied with their gadget and are unable to make them separate with them, instantly and regularly checking mobile or internet, sending SMS unnecessarily playing game all the time. Later on they are adapting maladaptive avoidance behavior, they are getting offline socially aloof or isolated. He further added in his article that there is a need to build boundaries, keeping in mind the new realities before diagnosing media users into disorder.

An Indian study by Akashdeep Bharadwaj, Vinay Avasthi, and Sam Goundar survey tries to analyse pattern of social networking usage in India youth in which they identify that these social networking sites are benefiting in cultural development, building self identity, developing relationships and acquisition of social, communication, and technical skills. They also identify the determinants of social networking addiction. They added that as compared to other countries Indian student's social network addiction exists.

A study by Fanni Banyai, Agnes Zsila, Orsolya Kiraly, Aniko Maraz, Zsuzanna Elekes, Mark D. Griffiths, Cecilie Schou Andressen, and Zsolt Demetrovics (2017) used Bergen Social Media Addiction Scale (BSMAS) and latent profile analysis found that approx 4.5% adolescents belong to at risk of social media addiction along with that they also report low self esteem and they were diagnosed with high level of depression symptoms. This research study concluded by suggesting different prevention and intervention programs such as content- control software, counselling, cognitive-behavioural therapy so forth.

In the article of Mark D Griffiths and Daria J Kuss (2017) describes that individuals who are fear of missing out (FOMO) are more likely to have social media addiction. Similarly, sometimes people feel the same thing appears to hold true of mobile phone use and fear of being without a mobile phone. Therefore the author concluded that people who are engaged in social networking shows active engagement in using mobile technologies, FOMO, nomophobia and mobile phone addiction appear to be associated with social networking site addiction.

Carolyn C.Morf & Frederick Rhodewalt article tries to explain dynamic self regulatory processing model of narcissism and exhibits supporting evidence. Author describes narcissists as insensitive to others' concerns and social constraints, narcissist persons describe other personalities as inferior, and their self regulatory efforts often are counterproductive. They say that there are some limitations in conceptualization, which give imprecise definition and controversial approaches to measurement of narcissism. In this article, the author believes that the process model of narcissism together with supporting validation research will help in providing a more appropriate definition of the construct. Author's work has been constructed on developing a self-regulatory processing model for the narcissistic personality that can be applied in understanding other categorical concepts of personality.

Rebecca L. Kauten, Christopher T. Barry (2015) their studies try to find a relation between adolescent narcissism and with different indices of prosocial behavior. They concluded their finding that non-pathological narcissism has positive relationship with parent related prosocial behavior same as grandiose narcissism have positive relation with both self and parent reported prosocial behavior. On the other hand vulnerable narcissism did not demonstrate a significant relation with any kind of variant of prosocial behavior. Therefore researchers define briefly that the relation between adolescent narcissism and pro-social behavior is based on the dimension of narcissism and the method of assessing prosocial behavior.

Article given by Michael D. Barnett and Kendall J. Sharp (2017) describes that among women, narcissism was associated with public and private self absorption whereas in men, narcissism was only associated with public self absorption. In relation between self absorption and narcissism they both were moderated by gender and they both share a component of pathological self focused attention.

Marta Maleszaa and Magdalena Claudia Kaczmarek (2018) defines two forms of narcissism which are titled as **grandiose narcissism** and **vulnerable narcissism, in** further study they identify correlation in which they found that vulnerable narcissism was negatively related to the stop reaction time, which can be concluded by saying that people high in vulnerable narcissism scored shorter stop reaction time value and thus consequently present less impulsive responding.

NPI 16- a study done by Daniel R. Ames, Paul Rose, Cameron P. Anderson (2005) who define abut NPI-16 and try to elaborate that why short NPI is Parallel to NPI-40. They concluded by saying that NPI-16 has notable face, internal, discriminant, and predictive validity and it positively serves alternative measures of narcissism when the situation is not in favour to measure on long and time taking inventories.

Tiffany A. Somerville indicates that several studies show that use of social media is mostly likely to exhibit narcissistic behavior. His study tries to find out how new forms of interaction affects psychological and emotional elements such through social media may be correlated with narcissistic traits in some way but not in a particularly strong manner. Social media use may increase narcissistic behavior for other reasons. It also shows a significant impact on self esteem. He ended his topic by indicating future scope in doing research in discovering how the effects of social media exposure have on adolescent self esteem.

Studies demonstrate that narcissistic people act, portray themselves and are perceived on different social media sites in the same manner as they are in their real life. Mediational analyses in this research done by Laura E. Buffardi and W. Keith Campbell

(2008) reveal that narcissistic people like the content on social networking sites are, quantity of social interaction, their photo self promotion, photo attractiveness.

Olga Paramboukis, Jason Skues and Lisa Wise, author's aims in this study is to examine the relationship between narcissism, self esteem, and instagram usages and to explore the reality of increasing narcissism due to excessive use of social media. Although it has been around 40yrs for inventing about narcissism and still there is ongoing debate about finding whether narcissism should be conceptualized as a psychiatrically diagnosed personality disorder or subclinical personality traits. This found that a common distinction in both the clinical and social/personality psychology literature is between grandiose and vulnerable narcissism. According to this study finding they have provided theoretical, methodologies and practical implications this study firstly provides further evidence for grandiose and vulnerable narcissism and these subtypes are differently related to self esteem. Secondly, study has tried to expand the research on narcissism subtype and different social networks. Concluding his study they found weak evidence for any relation between narcissism and instagram usage, social media giving rise to unprecedented narcissistic behavior are somewhat exaggerated despite some limitations of the study, the finding gives some better understanding of the topic.

For more deep understanding Cecilie Schou Andreassen, Stale Pallesen, Mark D. Griffiths (2016) conducted the study whose aim was to examine the association between addictive use of social media, narcissism and self esteem. Concluding their finding as establishing a positive relationship. Narcissists were associated with higher scores on BSMAS. Women scored higher on Social media addiction scales. Addictive social media use reflects a need to feed the ego and attempt to inhibit a negative self-evaluation.

Next significant study is by Kun-Hu Chen and Grace Ya (2010) whose aim of the study was to investigate the relationship between self identity and health related quality of life. He concluded that for better life experience of in-depth awareness of the self is very important. Campbell's (1990) finding that self-clarity and certainty are related to self-esteem, which, in turn, is an important negative correlate with depression in many other studies (Fenzel 1994; Harter and Marold 1992). In another study, Wu and Yao (2007) also indicated a positive relationship between self-certainty and adolescent quality of life while individuals perceived a higher sense of control.

In order to study the dynamics of self Yadollah Mehria, Seyed Mostafa Salaria, Milad Sabzeharaye Langroudi, Hamid Bahrami Zadeh (2011) conducted studies and try to describe self as it is a highly important psychological construct which helps in providing framework for understanding the world in better manner. They concluded that individuals who reported emotional instability had difficulty in maintaining a clear sense of self in a relationship, experiencing greatest interpersonal distress and other psychological problems. In contrast those who are better able to regulate their emotion, think clearly under stress, and stay in good emotional contact also maintain a clear sense of self which shows highest level or psychological and interpersonal well being. Long and Chen (2007) his study examines to identify the impact of internet usages on self identity development. The four dimensions of identity development are – decision making, identity formation, self reflection, and ego strength or fidelity. Researchers found positive relations among them.

In the study of Yadollah Mehri, Seyed Mostafa Salari, Milad Sabzeharaye Langroudi, Hamid Bahrami Zadeh (2011) identify the relationship between differentiation of self and aspects of identity. In which they found a positive relation that differentiation of self will positively influence on aspects of identity. Apart from that this study's correlation analysis shows that aspect of differential of self inventory(DSI) were negatively associated with aspect of identity questionnaire-IV (AIQ-IV)

An article given by Ania Molenda (2017) described collective identity that according to sociological definition, collective identity is about a group's common interest, experience and solidarities. It helps to express people's belonging, shared idea of political and cultural realm.

Jonathan M. Cheek and Stephen R. Briggs (1982) their study focuses on the relationship between social and personal aspects of identity with public and private self consciousness. They identify that public self consciousness is correlated significantly with the social aspect of identity and on other hand private self consciousness is correlated significantly with personal aspect of identity.

Yadollah Mehri, Seyed mostafa Salari, Milad Sabzeharaye Langroudi, and Hamid Bahramzadeh (2011) They study to find out the relationship between differentiation of self and aspect of identity (AIQ-IV). They identify with regression analyses that aspect of differentiation of self will influence aspects of identity. They concluded that individuals who were emotionally reactive and less able to regulate their emotions, having difficulty in maintaining a clear sense of self in relationship and who engage themselves either in emotional cut-off or fusion with others, experienced the greatest interpersonal distress and psychological problem. In contrast they also found that those who were better able to emotionally regulate, think clearly under stress, and stay in good emotional contact with others. They added that they maintained a clear sense of self in those relationships, reported the highest level of psychological and interpersonal well-being.

Chiara pattaro (2015) his article aims to investigate the discourse on youth identity and the role of new media in society. He says that social media is transforming the perception of the people. It is creating new path for social relations, affecting lifestyles, socialization and communication process and affecting the construction of identity

In the article of Michael Ermann (2004) demonstrate in his article on media identity that nowadays identity formation factors in human development are caused by communication through television, video and internet. Authors define media identity in the 21st century as a type of narcissistic socialization, under which there is experience of feelings and actions by denial of expression within the very relationships in which they are produced. In such a way social resignation has become the core and ideal feature of media identity.

The purpose of Virgil Zeigler-Hill and David R.C. Trombly (2018) study was to examine the connection between narcissism and mate value. This topic focuses on understanding how individuals view their romantic partners and themselves. They found that perceived partner mate value mediate the positive association that narcissistic admiration had with self perceived mate value as well as the negative association that narcissistic rivalry had with self perceived mate value.(RI)

W.Keith Campbell (2001) this article presents the social cognitive model of narcissism, given by Morf and Rhodewalt under which they define that narcissism is linked to the concept of self concept and interpersonal relationship. Further they added that narcissism can be functional and can be a healthy strategy in order to deal with the modern and advanced world.

Kali H. Ttrzesniewski, M. Brent Donnella, Richard W. Robins (2008) investigate in their research that in today's scenario in which young people have increasingly inflated their own impression of themselves as compared with their previous generation is a sort of doubt, because they found no such evidence on such respected topic of their investigation.

Carolyn C. Morf & Frederick Rhodewalt (2001) author casts narcissism as motivated self construction which is shaped by dynamic interaction of cognitive and affective intrapersonal processes and interpersonal self-regulatory strategies.

In identification of how leader charisma and constructive and destructive forms of narcissism interact to influence follower psychological empowerment and moral identity, John J. Sosik, Jae Uk Chun, Weichun Zhu (2013) says that their results revealed that there is a sort of positive relationship. They say that follower psychological empowerment mediates the differential interactive effects of leader charisma and constructive and destructive narcissism on follower moral identities. In the context of narcissism the author says that two forms of narcissism interact to influence followers' one is psychological empowerment and another is association with follower moral identities, which helps in better understanding. In order to define leaders' charisma, authors added by saying that, leaders who keep their ego checked and leaders who use their charisma to empower others they themselves become moral agents.

Chapter III
Method

CHAPTER-III
METHOD

3.1. Participants

Four hundred students between 15 to 29 years of age were chosen with an equal distribution of two hundred male and two hundred female were selected for my research study. The mean age of the sample was = 22; the mean age of male students was = 1.65; and for female students mean age was= 1.65. Their profiles contain additional information, such as educational qualification, place of permanent address (rural or urban), social category, economic status of family. Around hundred percent participants reported that they are having their own personal smartphone even with a laptop. My area of study is focused on Delhi and D-NCR.

3.2. Questionnaires

Three types of measures were administered; Bergen Social Media Addiction Scale and Aspects of Identity Questionnaire (AIQ). Questionnaire based Narcissistic Inventory Test with one subjective question at the end of questionnaire - "HOW IS YOUR EXPERIENCE WITH SOCIAL MEDIA? WRITE YOUR OPINION REGARDING SOCIAL MEDIA AND ITS EFFECT ON YOU". These questions were framed to define in the context of participants' self experiences, with interaction to social media.

3.2.1. Bergen Social Media Addiction Scale (BSMAS)

Bergen Social Media Addiction Scale (BSMAS) is a modified version of the previously validated Bergen Facebook Addiction Scale (BFAS; Andreassen et all.,2012). It is a six-item self report scale which was modified by using the term 'social media' instead of 'Facebook'. All questions contain a 5 point Likert scale spanning from Very rare (1) to Very often (5). The items correspond with diagnostic addiction criteria (American Psychiatric Association,1994). Six question having six core additional feature-

1) Salience 2) tolerance/ craving 3) mood modification 4) relapse/ loss of control 5) withdraw 6) conflict/ functional impairment.

Internal consistency of the BSMAS in the present study was Cronbach Alpha $\alpha=.78$

3.2.2. Narcissistic Personality Inventory-16 (NPI-16)

Narcissistic Personality Inventory-16 (NPI-16) is a shortened version of the original 40-items NPI (Raskin & Terry, 1988). The NPI-16 comprises 16 items assessing sub clinical narcissism (Ames, Rose, & Anderson, 2006). The NPI was basically developed by Raskin and Hall (1979) in order to measure narcissism as a personality trait in social psychological research. The development of NPI was based on the definition of narcissistic personality disorder found in the DSM-III, despite that, it is not used as a diagnostic tool for NPD and instead measures subclinical or normal expression of narcissism. Therefore we can say that those who get the highest possible score on the NPI do not necessarily have NPD. NPI-16 is unidimensional, hence there are no subscales.

Internal consistency of the NPI 16 in the present study was Cronbach Alpha $\alpha=.72$

3.2.3. Aspect of Identity (AIQ-IV)

The development of the Aspects of Identity Questionnaire (AIQ) began with the selection of items from Sampson's (1978) list of identity characteristics that were judged to represent the domains of personal and social identity (Cheek & Briggs, 1981, 1982). Subsequently, some items were reworded, others eliminated, and new items were developed to improve the reliability and content validity of the measures (Cheek, 1982/83; Cheek & Hogan, 1981; Hogan & Cheek, 1983). Psychometric analyses indicated that certain items originally scored in the social identity category (e.g., "Being a part of the many generations of my family") were tending to cluster on a third factor representing communal or collective identity. A third scale for this domain was developed (Cheek, Underwood, & Cutler, 1985) and has now been expanded (Cheek, Tropp, Chen, & Underwood, 1994). Neither the social nor collective scales focus on intimate relationships with close friends or romantic partners, so a fourth scale for relational identity orientation (‒Being a good friend to those I really care about") was added to the AIQ-IV (Cheek, Smith, & Tropp, 2002).

Four -factor model of AIQ is designed in order to study four different component of self identity which are given below-

1) Personal or individual self, which reflects our private beliefs about our psychological traits and abilities. (e.g., ‒My personal values and moral standards"). Internal consistency of the personal identity orientation in present study was Cronbach Alpha α=0.79

2) Relational self, which reflects how we see ourselves in the context of our intimate relationships. (e.g., ‒My relationship with the people I feel close to"). Internal consistency of the relationship identity orientation in the present study was Cronbach Alpha α=0.82

3) Social self, which reflects how we see ourselves in more general interpersonal contexts, including our social roles and reputation (i.e., self-presentation). (e.g., ‒My reputation, what others think of me"). Internal consistency of the social identity orientation in the present study was Cronbach Alpha α=0.77

4) Collective self, which reflects how we represent our various reference group identities. *(e.g., "My race or ethnic background")*. Internal consistency of the collective identity orientation in the present study was Cronbach Alpha α=0.74

5) Superficial self, which refers to a measure of an emphasis on surface qualities of self immediately visible to others. Internal consistency of the superficial identity orientation in the present study was Cronbach Alpha α=0.74

The number of items in the forms of Likert Scale spanning from **not important** (1) to **extremely important** (5) in each category are –

a) Personal Identity Orientation : 10 items

b) Relational Identity Orientation : 10 items

c) Social Identity Orientation : 7 items

d) Collective Identity Orientation : 8 Items

e) Special Items : 10 items

Research on the reliability and validity of the AIQ-IV questionnaire was only found in studies done abroad, nothing found in the context of India. Antonia and Marcia (2000) found reliability coefficients between 0.60 and 0.80 are acceptable. Cronbach alpha should be 0.70 or higher for a set of items to be considered acceptable (Nunnally & Bernstein, 1994).

Participant Characteristics
Total Participant = 400
Age Group = 15 TO 29 Yrs
Profession: Diversified as Much as Possible and Randomised
Sampling: Based on Simple Random Sampling
Questionnaire: Based on Three Psychometric Tests
1. NPI-16, 2. BSMA, 3. PI-SI-RI-CI-SP Test

3.2.4. Qualitative Analysis Tool Thematic Analysis

Qualitative researcher is often described as the research instrument insofar as his or her ability to understand, describe and interpret experiences and perceptions is key to uncovering meaning in particular circumstances and contexts.

Thematic Analysis – Thematic analysis is the process of identifying patterns or themes within qualitative data.

Braun & Clarke (2006) suggest that it is the first qualitative method that should be learned as _..it provides core skills that will be useful for conducting many other kinds of analysis' (p.78).

Thematic analysis (TA) is a widely used qualitative data analysis method. TA is a method that focuses on identifying patterned meaning across a dataset. In TA the aim or purpose is to identify patterns of meaning across a dataset that provide an answer to the research question being addressed. Now the question arises how patterns are identified, i.e. through a rigorous process of data familiarization, data coding, and theme development and revision. In TA questions are related to people's experiences or people's view and perceptions.

There are different ways of Thematic Analysis –

1) Inductive way – coding and theme development are directed by the content of the data.

2) Deductive way – coding and theme development are directed by existing concepts or ideas.

3) Semantic way – coding and theme development reflect the explicit content of the data.

4) Latent way – coding and theme development report concepts and assumptions underpinning the data.

5) Realist or essentialist way – focuses on reporting an assumed reality evident in the data.

6) Constructionist way – looking at how a certain reality is created by the data

The goal of a thematic analysis is to identify themes, i.e. patterns in the data that are important or interesting, and use these themes to address the research or say something about an issue. This is much more than simply summarising the data; a good thematic analysis interprets and makes sense of it. A common pitfall is to use the main interview questions as the themes (Clarke & Braun, 2013). Typically, this reflects the fact that the data have been summarised and organised, rather than analysed.

Braun & Clarke (2006) distinguish between two levels of themes: semantic and latent. Semantic themes *...within the explicit or surface meanings of the data and the analyst is not looking for anything beyond what a participant has said or what has been written.'* (p.84). The analysis in this worked example identifies themes at the semantic level and is representative of much learning and teaching work. We hope you can see that analysis moves beyond describing what is said to focus on interpreting and explaining it. In contrast, the latent level looks beyond what has been said and *...starts to identify or examine the underlying ideas, assumptions, and conceptualisations – and ideologies - that are theorised as shaping or informing the semantic content of the data'* (p.84).

Chapter IV
Results

CHAPTER-IV
RESULT

This chapter is organized into two parts, Part A explains ‗Quantitative Data Results' and Part B explains ‗Qualitative Data Results'

4.1. Part A: - Quantitative Data Results

The data obtained from the subjects were properly arranged and appropriately organized in the form of tabulation with respect to each of the factors or variables considered in the present study. Systematically presentation of the data has reflected the measures of the obtained selected study variables and their statistical distributions on the basis of which suitable statistical techniques were applied to analyze and to find out necessary information to serve the objectives of the study.

The fundamental point of this study is to reveal composite effect of social media on narcissism and identity. This chapter will present the finding of the study.

Table1: Demographic Details of the Participants

Demographic Variables	Mean	Std. Deviation
Gender	1.5000	.50063
Age-group	1.2175	.41306
Education	3.8350	.81205
Profession	1.0675	.32896
Residence	1.7600	.42762
Social-category	1.5050	.78519
Income	1.9650	.67075

Table showing demographic variables of the participants with their respective mean and standard deviation values.

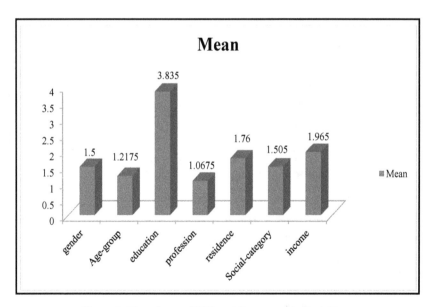

Figure 1: Mean Score of Different Demographic Variables

Table 2: Social Media, Narcissism and Dimensions of Identity; Mean and SD

Variables	Mean	SD
NPI	5.98	2.86
PI	39.05	6.24
RI	37.40	6.86
SI	22.63	5.17
CI	24.70	5.72
SP	32.43	5.89
SM	15.86	4.38

$N=400$, NPI- narcissistic personality inventory, SM- social media, PI- personal identity, RI- relational identity, SI- social identity, CI- collective Identity, SP- superficial identity

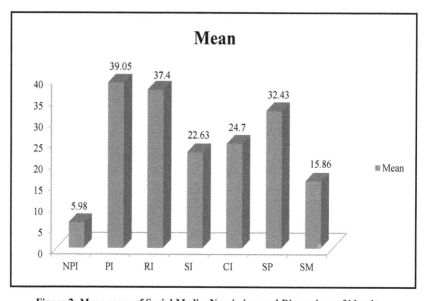

Figure 2: Mean score of Social Media, Narcissism and Dimensions of identity

NPI- narcissistic personality inventory, SM- social media, PI- personal identity, RI- relational identity, SI- social identity, CI- collective Identity, SP- superficial identity

Focusing on the findings according to the objectives,. First finding is to understand the nature and pattern of usage of social media among youth. The mean and standard deviation of social media user, narcissism and different aspects of identity are mentioned in table 2 and graphical portrayal has been described in figure 2.

Table 3: Usage of Social Media, Narcissism and Aspect of Identity: Mean, SD & T value, N=400

Variables	Low user (SM)		High user (SM)		t-value
	Mean	SD	Mean	SD	
NPI	5.68	2.82	6.39	2.85	2.02 *
PI	39.93	6.25	38.01	6.60	2.41 **
RI	38.44	6.83	37.02	7.35	1.61
SI	21.71	5.25	23.32	5.15	2.50 **
CI	24.09	5.15	24.62	5.77	0.79
SP	31.56	5.34	33.15	6.25	2.20 *

N=400, *p<0.05,(two tailed),significant,**p<0.01,(two tailed),significant, NPI- narcissistic personality inventory, SM- social media, PI- personal identity, RI- relational identity, SI- social identity, CI- collective Identity, SP- superficial identity

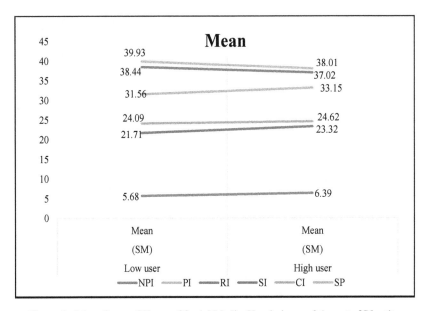

Figure 3: Mean Score of Usage of Social Media, Narcissism and Aspect of Identity

NPI- narcissistic personality inventory, SM- social media, PI- personal identity, RI- relational identity, SI- social identity, CI- collective Identity, SP- superficial identity

In order to investigate the impact of social media usage that is based on lower user and higher user on narcissism and different aspect of identity, Mean, SD, and t value has been identified. Under table 3 which highest mean score of the higher user of social media is narcissism, social identity, superficial identity on the other hand highest mean score of the lower user of social media is personal identity and relationship identity. The graphical portrayal of the mean is shown in figure 3.

Table 4: Correlation Patterns of Social media, Identity and Narcissism, N=400

	NPI	SM	PI	RI	SI	CI	SP
NPI	1	.099*	-.178**	-.121*	.091	-.020	.022
SM		1	-.133**	-.081	.120*	.020	.105*
PI			1	.574**	.207**	.110*	.263**
RI				1	.234**	.120*	.218**
SI					1	.369**	.482**
CI						1	.457**
SP							1

$N=400$, *$p<0.05$,(two tailed),significant,**$p<0.01$,(two tailed),significant, NPI- narcissistic personality inventory, SM- social media, PI- personal identity, RI- relational identity, SI- social identity, CI- collective Identity, SP- superficial identity\

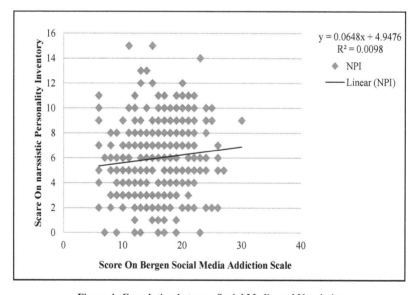

Figure 4: Correlation between Social Media and Narcissism

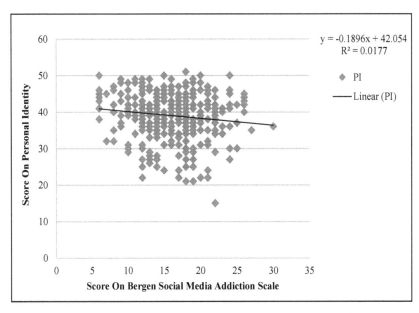

Figure 5: Correlation Between social Media And Personal Identity

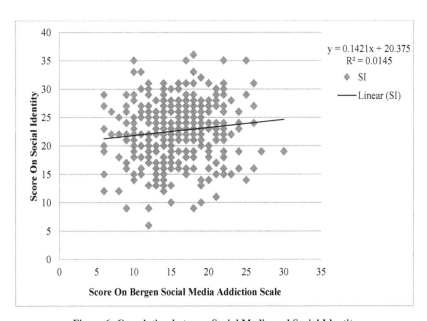

Figure 6: Correlation between Social Media and Social Identity

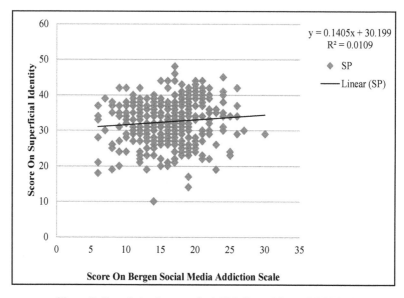

Figure 7: Correlation between Social Media and Superficial Identity

The correlation coefficient between the usage of social media, narcissism and different aspect of identity has been identified with the help of Pearson product moment correlation which is presented in table 3 under that it clearly shows both positive and negative relationships. Results indicate that On the dimensions of narcissism it is positively significant with social media with r =.099 p< 0.05 (significant two tailed) and on the other hand negatively significant with personal identity r = -0.178 p<0.01 and relationship identity r = -0.121 p< 0.05 focusing on the social media it is positively significant with narcissism r = 0.099 p < 0.05, social identity r = 0.120 p < 0.05 and superficial identity r = 0.105 p < 0.05 on the other side negatively significant with personal identity r = -0.133 p < 0.01 On the first sub-dimension of self identity ie. personal identity which have positively significant relationship with relationship identity r = 0.574 p <0.01, social identity r = 0.207 p < 0.01 superficial identity r = 0.263 p < 0.01 and collective identity r = 0.110 p < 0.05

and having significantly negative relationship with narcissism r = -0.178 and social media r = -0.133 both at the same level p < 0.01 On the second sub-dimension ie. relationship identity having a positive significant relationship with personal identity r = 0.574, social identity r = 0.234, superficial identity r = 0.218 all three are respectively significant at the level of p < 0.01, and collective identity r = 0.12 p < 0.05 level and having significantly negative relationship with narcissistic personality inventory r = -0.121 p < 0.05 In social identity they have been positively significant relationship with social media r = 0.120 p < 0.05, rest self identity aspects are significant i.e. personal identity r = 0.207, relationship identity r = 0.234, collective identity r = 0.369 and superficial identity r = 0.482 at the level of p <0.01 level In respect to collective identity its significantly positively related with personal identity r = 0.110, relationship identity r = 0.120 both at the same level which is p < 0.05, rest other social identity r = 0.369, and superficial identity r = 0.457 p < 0.01 along with reversely and significantly related with narcissistic personality inventory In aspect of superficial identity it has positive and significantly related with social media r = 0.105 p < 0.05, where as personal identity r =0.263, relationship identity r =0.218, social identity r = 0.482, and collective identity r =0.457.

Table 5: Regression Coefficient Model for Outcome Variable Social Media from Pridictors

Predictors	R	R²	R²	β	t
NPI	0.099	0.010	0.007	0.099	1.986*
PI	0.133	0.018	0.015	0.133	0.008**
SI	0.120	0.014	0.012	0.120	2.418**
SP	0.105	0.011	0.008	0.105	2.097*

Table 5- shows regression analysis of predictors narcissistic personality inventory, Personal Identity, Social Identity and Superficial identity. The significant predictors came out to be Narcissism with R equal to (0.099).R square equal to (0.010) and Adjusted R square equal to (0.007). The contribution of Narcissism are statistically significant as reveal by ß equal to (0.099, p = 0.04) at 0.05 levels.

The significant predictors came out to be personal identity with R equal to (0.133). R square equal to (0.018) and Adjusted R square equal to equal to (0.015). The contribution of personal identity are statistically significant as reveal by ß equal to (0.133, p = 0.008) at 0.01 levels.

The significant predictors came out to be social identity with R equal to (0.120). R square equal to (0.014) and Adjusted R square equal to (0.012). The contribution of social identity are statistically significant as found by ß equal to (0.120, p = 0.01) at 0.01 levels.

The significant predictors came out to be superficial identity with R equal to (0.105). R square equal to (0.011) and Adjusted R square equal to (0.008). The contribution of superficial identity are statistically significant as found by ß equal to (0.105, p = 0.037) at 0.05 levels.

Table 6: Correlation Patterns of Social Media, Identity and Narcissism, High Users, N=148

	NPI	SM	PI	RI	SI	CI	SP
NPI	1	.026*	-.083	-.038	.100	.045	.100
SM		1	-.025*	.038	.003*	-.042	.045*
PI			1	.577**	.281**	.166*	.273**
RI				1	.337**	.217**	.315**
SI					1	.401**	.535**
CI						1	.469**
SP							1

N=100, *p<0.05,(two tailed),significant,**p<0.01,(two tailed),significant, NPI- narcissistic personality inventory, SM- social media, PI- personal identity, RI- relational identity, SI- social identity, CI- collective Identity, SP- superficial identity

Table 6 shows User wise analysis of the correlation between narcissistic personality inventory, social media, and different aspect of identity are depicted here which shows how higher social media user responses are related to each on that regarding with the help of Pearson correlation. As shown in table 4 social media is positively and significantly related to narcissism r = 0.026 at the level of p <0.05 personal identity were positively significant relationship with relationship identity r = 0.577, social identity r = 0.281, superficial identity r = 0.273 at the level of p < 0.01 and at the level of p = < 0.05 personal identity is significantly related with collective identity with r = 0.166 In the sphere of relationship identity it has been positively significant relationship with personal identity r = 0.577, social identity r = 0.337, collective identity r = 0.217, relationship identity r = 315 in this aspect of identity all the correlation relationship are related to each other at the level of p < 0.01 Focusing towards the other area of identity that is social identity which is significantly positive related to personal identity r =0.281, relationship identity r =0.337 , collective identity r =0.401, superficial identity r =0.535 all are significant at the level of p < 0.01 In collective identity it shows positive significant related with personal identity r = 0.166 p< 0.05, relationship identity r =0.217 social identity r =0.401 superficial identity r = 0.469 rest all three identity are significant at level of p< 0.01 In superficial identity like other aspect of identity it is also positively significant related to the rest of the identity such as personal identity r = 0.273, relationship identity r =0.315, social identity r = 0.535, collective identity r =0.469 all are significant at the same level p<0.01

Table 7: Correlation Patterns of Social Media, Identity and Narcissism; Low Users, N=119

	NPI	SM	PI	RI	SI	CI	SP
NPI	1	.074*	-.175	-.107	.003	-.291**	-.139
SM		1	-.196*	-.197*	.037	.039	.075
PI			1	.633**	.219*	.049	.219*
RI				1	.219*	.070	.152
SI					1	.278**	.442**
CI						1	.396**
SP							1

N=100, *p<0.05,(two tailed),significant,**p<0.01,(two tailed),significant,NPI- narcissistic personality inventory, SM- social media,PI- personal identity, RI- relational identity, SI- social identity, CI- collective Identity, SP- superficial identity

Table 7 summarizes the result of correlation with narcissism, social media and different aspect of self identity within the low users. On the basis of that it has been identified that narcissistic personality inventory is positively significant with social media $r = 0.074$ at the level of $p<0.05$ and is reversely significant related to collective identity $r = -0.291$ $p <0.01$, in relation with social media it is negatively significant related with personal identity $r = -0.196$ and relationship identity $r = -0.197$ both of them are significant at the same level which is $p<0.01$ Focusing on the aspect of identity, on the first aspect that is personal identity which is having significantly positively relationship with relationship identity $r = 0.219$ $p < 0.01$, social identity $r =0.219$ and superficial identity $r = 0.219$ both t $p < 0.05$ on the other hand it is also negatively significantly related with social media $r = -0.176$ at the level of $p < 0.05$ On the second aspect of identity that is relationship identity which is significantly positively related with personal identity $r = 0.633$ $p < 0.01$ social identity $r = 0.219$ $p < 0.05$ along with significantly negatively related with social media $r = -0.197$ $p< 0.05$

On the dimension of social identity it is positively significantly related with personal identity r = 0.219 relationship identity r = 0.219 both personal and relationship identity are significant at the level of p < 0.05 and social identity r = 0.278 collective identity r = 0.278 both are significant at p < 0.01 level In relation with collective identity it defines that it is positively significant related with social identity r = 0.278 and superficial identity r = 0.396 both at the level of 0.01 beside that it is reversely significantly related with narcissistic personality inventory r = -0.291 p < 0.01 on the last subdimention of aspect of identity that is superficial identity which is positively significantly related with personal identity r = 0.219 p< 0.05, social identity r = 0.442 collective identity r = 0.396 both re significant at the level of p < 0.01

Table 8: Comparison between Males and Females on Social Media, Identity and Narcissism: Mean, SD & t value, N=400

Variables	Males		Females		t-value
	Mean	SD	Mean	SD	
NPI	6.61	2.75	5.34	2.85	4.54**
SM	16.02	4.38	15.69	4.39	0.75
PI	37.10	6.48	41.00	5.32	6.59**
RI	36.01	7.20	39.10	6.20	4.15**
SI	22.47	5.27	23.89	5.08	0.61
CI	25.10	5.94	24.44	5.48	0.91
SP	32.10	6.04	33.10	5.70	1.66

N=400, *p<0.05,(two tailed),significant,**p<0.01,(two tailed),significant, NPI- narcissistic personality inventory, SM- social media, PI- personal identity, RI- relational identity, SI- social identity, CI- collective Identity, SP- superficial identity

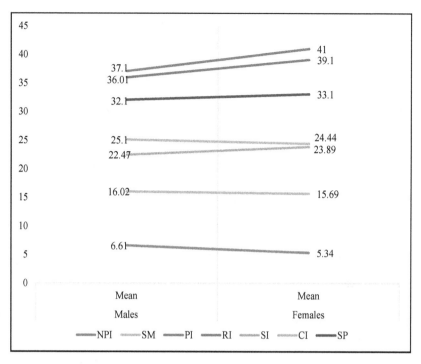

Figure 8: Mean Comparison between Males and Females on Social Media, Identity and Narcissism: N=400

NPI- narcissistic personality inventory, SM- social media, PI- personal identity, RI- relational identity, SI- social identity, CI- collective Identity, SP- superficial identity

The mean and standard deviation score for the male and female shows that male participants are more narcissistic than female, on other hand female are more inclined towards personal identity and relationship identity as shown in the table no 8, figure 8

Table 9: Comparison between males and females on Social media, Identity and Narcissism: Mean, SD & t value, High Users N=148

Variables	Male		Female		T-value
	Mean	SD	Mean	SD	
NPI	6.74	2.73	6.01	2.95	1.56
PI	36.23	6.54	40.00	6.13	3.60**
RI	35.39	7.57	38.84	6.68	2.91**
SI	22.65	5.61	24.07	4.54	1.67*
CI	24.96	6.17	24.25	5.32	0.73
SP	31.89	6.78	34.55	5.29	2.63**

N=100, *$p<0.05$,(two tailed),significant,**$p<0.01$,(two tailed),significant, NPI- narcissistic personality inventory, SM- social media, PI- personal identity, RI- relational identity, SI- social identity, CI- collective Identity, SP- superficial identity

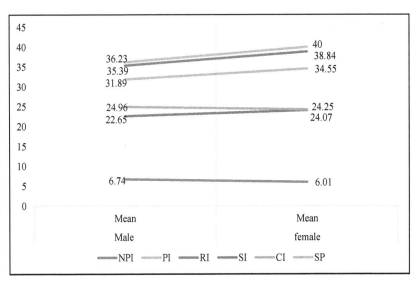

Figure 9: Mean Comparison between Males and Females on Social Media, Identity and Narcissism: High Users N=148

The mean and standard deviation score for the male and female shows on social media higher user that female are significantly high on personal identity, relationship identity, social identity and superficial identity as shown in the table no 9, figure 9.

Table 10: Comparison between Males and Females on Social Media, Identity and Narcissism: Mean, SD & T value, Low Users N=119

Variables	Male		Female		t-value
	Mean	SD	Mean	SD	
NPI	6.25	2.66	5.20	2.88	2.05*
PI	37.43	7.22	42.07	4.30	4.32**
RI	36.90	8.00	39.76	5.37	2.31*
SI	20.90	5.38	22.40	5.10	1.55
CI	23.52	5.45	24.57	4.86	1.11
SP	30.50	6.03	32.46	4.51	2.02*

$N=100$, *$p<0.05$,(two tailed),significant,**$p<0.01$,(two tailed),significant, NPI- narcissistic personality inventory, SM- social media, PI- personal identity, RI- relational identity, SI- social identity, CI- collective Identity, SP- superficial identity

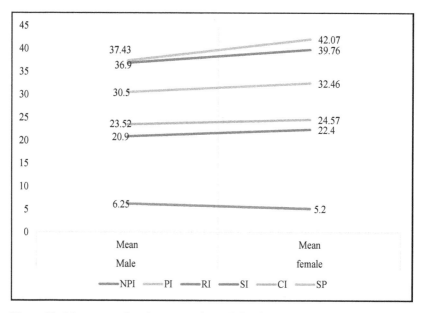

Figure 10: Mean comparison between males and females on Social media, Identity and narcissism: Low Users N=119

The mean and standard deviation score for the male and female shows on social media low user that male participants are more narcissistic than female, on other hand female are more inclined towards personal identity, relationship identity and superficial identity as shown in the table no 10, figure 10.

4.2. Part B:- Qualitative Data Result

S. No.	Themes	Subthemes	Verbatim
1	salience	Feeling captivated, Impulsive reactions, Binge thinking, Expansion of ideas,	"It helps to create good mindset" "Social media ka prayog sakaratmak dhang se karne ke karan mujhpe sakaratmak prabhav pada hai………"
2	tolerance	Loneliness, Urge, craving	"I can't even complete my daily task without using it." "my brain usually get stuck when people ask me to do something other than social media……i don't feel any interest in other area."
3	mood modification	Escaping reality, Unrealistic expectations, Aloofness, looking forward for temporary solutions. Stressful life experience, escape Negative self apprehension.	"It helps me to forget my personal problems and other issues which I face throughout the day. In fact, it helps me to run away from the harsh realities and negative vibes in life. But at the same time it also has bad impact like waste of time, energy etc. but at the end of the day it is also about helping yourself to forget about all the other things and moving with the generation." "it's easy to make your self occupied rather focusing on useless and irrelevant stuffs"
4	Relapse	Self control/ determination, Loss of control	"When I have like no work to do, I get deeply involved in the social media and it harm me both physically and mentally, physically it give me severe headache and mentally I think about the stuff continuously. So I want to use it upto a certain limit but it is my hard luck that I can't control using social media up to very extent." "Social Media makes me less of concentrated or you can say I am too much attractive towards mobile phone or computer."

S. No.	Themes	Subthemes	Verbatim
5	Withdrawal	Maladjustment, Compulsive behaviour, Ostentatious,	"From my point of view it's a good platform of how to be popular on this media, which makes you more famous than you are. If you have so special "things" which are required according to demand."
			"I become addicted to it, most often it has affected my eyes"
6	Conflict	Inability to manage time, Time spend on social media, functional impairment	"I indulge in social media more as stress buster, but sometimes find it hard to get my work done on time due to it, it affects somewhat negatively when I have a lot to do, and I use social media to procrastinate."
			"There was a time when I was addicted to social media spending hour's online caused eye strain, stress and lack of sleep."
7	Self Identity	Self identity crisis, need for belongingness, Way of expression of ideas, Self recognition, Bullying, Online harassment	"I spend lots of good times on social media with my friends. So, as professionally and emotionally it is good for me. But sometimes when I spend excessive time on social media, I found some type of problem like, I waste my time and didn't concentrate on my studies."
			"It definitely provide a platform to express yourself as an individual but also plays an important role in an individual's thoughts about oneself"
			Some people try to exaggerate themselves
8	Narcissism	Positive experience, Self Verification, Self Confirmation Bias	"I am loving it"
			"Sharing is good"
			"Easy to get famous"
			"I love sharing my photos, videos, and doing live chatting with my fans, it gives me recognition all over the world".

Each of the themes had subtheme, which was framed on the basis of responses given by the participants, emerge to further explicate the findings on which regard have selected specific one or two examples so that appropriate and authentic explanation can be given which also help in order to develop in additionally explain the discoveries on which respect have chosen explicit a couple of models with the goal that fitting and bona fide clarification can be given

Theme 1 - Salience

According to theme Subthemes were framed which are, Feeling captivated, Impulsive reactions, Binge thinking, Expansion of ideas. Some of the examples on which theme and subthemes were formulated are-

"It helps to create good mindset"

"Social media ka prayog sakaratmak dhang se karne ke karan mujhpe sakaratmak prabhav pada hai........."

According to wikipedia - The **salience** (also called **saliency**) of an item is the state or quality by which it stands out from its neighbors. Saliency detection is considered to be a key attentional mechanism that facilitates learning and survival by enabling organisms to focus their limited perceptual and cognitive resources on the most pertinent subset of the available sensory data. (*salience in cognitive neuroscience).* The Oxford English Dictionary defines salience as "most noticeable or important.

Bryn Farnsworth, Ph.D, September 11th, 2018, Share his idea on blog titled "Saliency in Human Behavior Research" while defining salience he identity factors which falls into three categories: Properties of the stimulus itself, how the stimulus fits with its context, and the internal cognitive state of the observer. Salience is usually produced by novelty or unexpectedness, but can also be brought about by shifting one's attention to that feature. The term salient refers to anything (person, behavior, trait, etc.) that is prominent, conspicuous, or otherwise noticeable compared with its surroundings (Taylor, S. E., & Fiske, S. T. 1978)

Theme 2 - Tolerance

Subthemes are, Loneliness, Urge, craving. Some of the examples are –

"I can't even complete my daily task without using it."

"my brain usually get stuck when people ask me to do something other than social media......i don't feel any interest in other area."

Beginning with Wikipedia definitions:

Tolerance is define as a fair, objective, and permissive attitude toward those whose opinions, practices, race, religion, nationality, etc., differ from one's own; freedom from bigotry.

According to APA dictionary of psychology in *DSM–IV–TR*, a cluster of cognitive, behavioral, and physiological symptoms indicating continued use of a substance despite significant substance-related problems. There is a pattern of repeated substance ingestion resulting in tolerance, withdrawal symptoms if use is suspended, and an uncontrollable drive to continue use

Theme 3 - mood modification

Subthemes are - Escaping reality, Unrealistic expectations, Aloofness, looking forward for temporary solutions. Stressful life experience, escape, Negative self apprehension. Some of the examples are –

"It helps me to forget my personal problems and other issues which I face throughout the day. In fact, it helps me to run away from the harsh realities and negative vibes in life. But at the same time it also has bad impact like waste of time, energy etc. but at the end of the day it is also about helping yourself to forget about all the other things and moving with the generation."

For mood modification people utilize the Internet all the time so as to change their negative mindset or to escape a negative mood from regular day to day existence (Greenfield, 2000; Vas and Gombor, 2008). Accordingly, utilizing the Internet to adjust state of mind may not really lead to negative results related with inclination for online social cooperation, over the top and enthusiastic use, and encountering mental withdrawal (Widyanto and Griffiths, 2006).

Theme 4 – relapse

Subthemes are - Self control, self determination, Loss of control. Some of the examples are –

―When I have like no work to do, I get deeply involved in the social media and it harm me both physically and mentally, physically it give me severe headache and mentally I think about the stuff continuously. So I want to use it up to a certain limit but it is my hard luck that I can't control using social media up to very extent."

Relapse happens when indications of a condition return. This occurs after a period without any indications. For instance, an individual with sadness may get alleviation from medicine or treatment. In any case, they may begin demonstrating indications again following a couple of long stretches of treatment. In the domain of dependence, relapse is an arrival to substance use after a time of nonuse. It is normal and can be normal during the troublesome procedure of progress. Somewhere in the range of 40% and 60% of people relapse inside their first year of treatment. Relapse is anything but an indication of bombed recuperation. Recuperation from fixation requires huge changes in way of life and conduct, running from changing companion circles to growing new ways of dealing with stress. It includes exploring another and new way.

The danger of relapse is most prominent in the initial 90 days of recuperation, a period when affectability to push is upgraded while affectability to remunerate is low and it might be enticing to fall again into natural examples of conduct.

Theme 5 – withdrawal

Subthemes are - Maladjustment, Compulsive behaviour, Ostentatious, Some of the examples are–

> "From my point of view it's a good platform of how to be popular on this media, which makes you more famous than you are. If you have so special "things" which are required according to demand."

> "I become addicted to it, most often it has affected my eyes"

Withdraw is defined at the point when a living being (doesn't need to be a human; can be another sort of creature) gets dependent on a substance, and afterward, they are kept from having that substance for an all-inclusive timeframe, they experience a time of withdrawal. A withdrawal condition is one of the pointers of a reliance disorder. It is likewise the characterizing normal for the smaller psycho-pharmacological importance of reliance.

Theme 6 – conflict

Subthemes are - Inability to manage time, Time spend on social media, functional impairment

Some of the example are –

> "I indulge in social media more as stress buster, but sometimes find it hard to get my work done on time due to it, it affects somewhat negatively when I have a lot to do, and I use social media to procrastinate."

"There was a time when I was addicted to social media spending hour's online caused eye strain, stress and lack of sleep."

conflict is an extremely normal term, in brain research, it alludes to whenever you have contradicting or incongruent activities, goals, or thoughts, you have strife. Conflict can be between two individuals, nations, gatherings, or even inside one individual (an interior clash). Conflict is dangerous and must be tended to so as to have tranquility, efficiency, or concordance.

Theme 7 – Self Identity

Subtheme are - Self identity crisis, need for belongingness, Way of expression of ideas, Self recognition, Bullying, Online harassment

Some of the example are –

> "I spend lots of good times on social media with my friends. So, as professionally and emotionally it is good for me. But sometimes when I spend excessive time on social media, I found some type of problem like, I waste my time and didn't concentrate on my studies."

> "It definitely provide a platform to express yourself as an individual but also plays an important role in an individual's thoughts about oneself"

Self-identity comprises a number of "self-images" that lie on a continuum, with personalised self-schemata at one extreme and self-characteristics related to social categories at the other (Hagger, Anderson, Kyriakaki, Darkings, 2007). Where some people try to exaggerate themselves.

Theme 8 - Narcissism

Subtheme are –

Narcissistic personality, Positive experience

Some of the examples are –

"I am loving it"

"Sharing is good"

"Easy to get famous"

Narcissism is when an individual develops the exaggerated feelings of self-importance, self-loving and excessively high self-esteem. Besides, in combination with these, it is a personality trait that is characterized with low empathy towards others.

CHAPTER-V
DISCUSSION AND INTERPRETATION

The aim of the study is to reveal a composite effect of social media, narcissism and self-identity. The preceding chapter presented the result of this study. The results show how social media, narcissism and self identity affect each other. The present chapter is to discuss the findings of the study.

H0 1 – Higher Social media users will show higher scores on narcissism.

Pearson correlations were used in this study to determine the relationship between Social Media and Narcissism with its different dimensions, Personal Identity, Relationship Identity, Social Identity, Collective Identity and Superficial Identity.

The first hypothesis states that Higher Social media users will show higher scores on narcissism, results indicated a significant positive correlation between social media and narcissism which depicts that excessive use of social media will lead to develop a higher narcissistic tendency.

Getting support from Qualitative analysis Verbatim like, ―easy to get famous", ―I love sharing my photos, videos, and doing live chatting with my fans, it gives me recognition all over the world".

We can not claim Social media as a neutral platform, it has a powerful effect in tapping into people's desire to see or shape themselves in their own terms. Higher urge of defining their own self and the competition that has occurred by the concept of social media, the meaning of endless elements has been changed. More examples can be defined with a good example which can be beauty in the current scenario. Because of this issue, the ratio in plastic surgeries and editing the photos has been increased a lot. More interestingly it can be understood by how people present themselves in a very effective and acceptable manner. This idea of behavior can be understood by the concept of "Self- Verification".

Self-verification theory proposes that people prefer to be seen as they see themselves, even if their self-views are negative (Swann 2012). Self-verification theory is based on the premise that individuals want to affirm and thus stabilize their firmly held self-views. This idea was first articulated by Prescott Lecky (1945) who proposed that chronic self-views give people a strong sense of coherence. Self-verification theory (Swann 1983) developed Lecky's idea that stable self-view organize people's efforts to maximize coherence. Supporting qualitative analysis theme and verbatim is-

Salience - "It definitely provide a platform to express yourself as an individual but also plays an important role in an individual's thoughts about oneself"

Withdrawal- "From my point of view it's a good platform for how to be popular on this media, which makes you more famous than you are. If you have special "things" which are required according to demand."

Self Absorption - For the reason given above, it clearly shows that people have a powerful desire to confirm themselves, thus consequently, it shows that individuals have strong craving to affirm. Article given by Michael D.Barnett and Kendall J. Sharp (2017) describes their results under study suggesting that self-absorption and narcissism share a component of pathological self-focused attention, and that a dysregulated status-seeking mechanism may be involved in narcissism.

There have been a number of conceptualizations of pathological self awareness (Raskin & Hall, 1979; Wink, 1991) and maladaptive self focused attention (McKenzie & Hoyle, 2008; Pincus et al., 2009). Narcissism may be conceptualized as a pathological form of self-focused attention (Raskin & Hall, 1979; Wink, 1991). This maladaptive self-focused attention is a characteristic that can be seen in both self-absorption and narcissism scales (McKenzie & Hoyle, 2008; Pincus et al., 2009). In this study, we sought to explore the links between the maladaptive self-focused attention found in self-absorption and narcissism.

Self Identity - ―It definitely provide a platform to express yourself as an individual but also plays an important role in an individual's thoughts about oneself‖

Self verification biased/ confirmation bias – a study done by Abdallah Alsaad, Abdallah Taamneh, Mohamad Noor Al-Jedaiah (2018) they try to find out the connection between increased rate of racist, hate crimes and hateful behavior. This research focuses on the relationship between social media and confirmation bias. Confirmation bias predicts that human beings have an unconscious propensity to search for, favor, recall, and interpret information in a way that confirms their previous beliefs and hypotheses, while giving disproportionately less attention to alternative possibilities which leads to polarization in beliefs.

Classic research in the selective exposure paradigm (Lazarsfeld, Berelson, & Gaudet, 1944) has demonstrated that people tend to prefer information that is consistent with their preexisting attitudes (―confirmation bias;‖ Hart et al., 2009). As a potential explanation of attitude-consistent choices, many studies refer to cognitive dissonance theory (Festinger, 1957), which states that inconsistencies in one's beliefs arouse mental discomfort: large body of research (e.g., Kunda, 1990) has shown that people are often driven to preserve their self-concept or worldviews, which may happen consciously or unconsciously with the illusion of still being objective.

Due to social media they can easily observe others' recommendations and evaluations of the content that is specific selective exposure to information towards their pre-conceived notion.It also supports with the idea that in people's freedom of choice are resulting into the selection of content that is likely to strengthen their initial viewpoints but on other hand it's unlikely to enhance their knowledge (Iyengar &Hahn, 2009; Stroud, 2011). Selective exposure online has also supported the notion of attitude-consistent choices (e.g., Garrett, 2009a; Knobloch-Westerwick & Meng, 2009).

Notorious confirmation bias is the result of self absorption and self verification which make people satisfy their self view. It becomes more adverse in context to narcissism. Such kind of disoriented and selective content is making people more narcissistic, which results into bad decision making and motivating human right violation.

Human rights violation – there are two types of narcissism grandiose and vulnerable. A study done by rebecca l. Kauten, Christopher t. Barry (2015) tries to identify the relation between adolescent narcissism and with different indices of pro and anti social behaviour. Results identified that grandiose narcissism has a positive relation with pro-social behaviour and vulnerable narcissism has positive relation with anti-social behaviour. A study done by Anna Z.Czarna, Marcin Zajenkowski, Oliwia Machiantowicz & Kinga Szymaniak (2019). The significant relationships between both forms of narcissism with aggression, hostility, anger and poor emotional managing. (form might be different) Findings suggest that narcissism is positively related to social media platforms significantly moderated the results and tend to become more violent. A study done by Jessica L. McCain and W. Keith Campbell (2018)

It has been clearly mentioned that latest crimes which are related to social media misinformation and fake news no country is equipped to deal with such kind of crimes

A social media post on Prophet Muhammad led to violence in Karnataka's Bengaluru on Tuesday. Major violence broke out in DJ Halli area after the protesters alleged that Congress MLA R Akhanda Srinivas Murthy's kin had allegedly uploaded a derogatory post about Prophet Muhammad on his Facebook account. The Maharashtra state administration is still trying to come to terms with the shocking lynching on 1 July 2020 in Dhule district in northern Maharashtra, where a restive mob of 3,500-plus villagers gathered outside the gram panchayat office in Rainpada village, broke open the locks, and killed five agricultural labourers on the suspicion that they were ‗child-lifters'. There have been 14 incidents of mob lynching and vigilante justice—fuelled by rumours spread on social media—in Maharashtra alone in less than a month since 8 June.

In 2012, for instance, a rumour that spread like wildfire on social media had the north-eastern people in Bengaluru fleeing the city overnight. ―These were not just random rumours, these are targeted. For example, the messages circulated in Bengaluru targeted Hindi-speaking migrants," said Pranesh Prakash, fellow at the Centre for Internet and Society, a Bengaluru-based think tank.

This was done through the lens of the Expectation Confirmation Biasness. Social Media is providing a platform where every performance is posited to follow an Expectation Confirmation Theory framework, in which social media users are either satisfied or dissatisfied depending on their subjective evaluation of performance.

H0 2 - Excessive use of social media will create dissociated self identity

Whenever we talk about self identity, it means how any person is recognizing or knowing himself in terms of ground base reality. It also refers to a balanced state of identification in respect to personal, relationship, social and collective identity. For my study I have chosen one other orientation of identity is superficial identity. With this identity it will help to understand the user's perception towards their identity formation influenced by social media. Lots of studies done to identify whether there is any relationship between social media and self identity formation impacted by social media. A study done by Madison Ganda (2014) identifies a relationship between identity development within online and offline social networking sites. In which they identify that there is no significant relationship.

Self is a person's essential being which distinguishes them from others especially in terms of introspection or reflexive action whereas Identity orientations refer to the relative importance that individuals place on various identity attributes or characteristics when constructing their self-definitions (Cheek, 1989). When we describe self identity it means how any person is recognizing or knowing himself in terms of ground base reality. Because, these different self-identity aspects can impact social behaviors in various ways (Ellemers, Spears & Doosje, 2002). Depending on which self-identity aspect is triggered, it may cause different behaviours and characteristics to surface. In the present study we have considered five different identity characteristics representing different domains of a person's self identity. Now a days where everyone has exposure to social media and they use social media platforms to understand themselves better, which directly affects people's perception of themselves.

Results show that in different domains of self-identity there is a positive and significant relationship between social media, personal identity, social identity and superficial identity.

The kind of relationship showing in the result table depicts that as social media will increase personal identity will decrease.

The line between the real person (or the "offline" one) and her projection onto social networking sites (her "online" self) is becoming blurred.(S. Hongladarom) due to which personal Identity is framing into personal identity deception which has become an increasingly important issue in the social media environment, where identity is forming without non verbal cues or artificial non verbal cues. Michail Tsikerdekis and Sherali Zeadally in his study he called it identity deception.(superficial identity).

Superficial identity- Under this study I found a significant positive relationship between social media and superficial identity. Reasons were found that, when a person is inclined towards addictive use of social media then the user's self disclosure (Self-disclosure refers to the process of revealing personal, intimate information about oneself to others.) quality deteriorates in the real world which leads towards feelings of loneliness which leads towards identity gaps hence lack of social support builds superficial identity (Jessica L. Rhodes 2014.)

Qualitative analysis supports by the theme and verbatim

> "it's easy to make yourself occupied rather focusing on useless and irrelevant stuffs"
> "It helps me to forget my personal problems and other issues which I face throughout the day. In fact, it helps me to run away from the harsh realities and negative vibes in life."

Social identity - significant positive relationship between social media and social identity supports the idea that society and new society is using technology undoubtly for their betterment. All these sites claims to make world open and connected, it brings people more close together, it helps in building common understanding. It is helping people to build community, a meaningful systematic change are happening around the world

Qualitative analysis supports by the theme and verbatim like-

"social media has provide me to be in touch of all my friends",

"provide lots of news and information",

"helps us to connect with the people around us",

"i am social keeda"

The reason can be that society and new society is using technology undoubtly for their betterment. These social media tools actually created something very beneficial in the world. They are working to unite lost friends and families. All these sites claim to make the world open and connected, it brings people more close together, it helps in building common understanding. It is helping people to build community, and meaningful systematic changes are happening around the world (being local connect global), and this is what I found in my study by getting a significantly positive relationship between social media and social identity.

Looking towards the actual fact we can say that social media tools are being used for changing society fundamentally. Social media is being used for manipulating human behavior. Under this study I found significant positive relationship between social media and superficial identity reason were found was that, when person is inclined towards addictive use of social media then user's self disclosure quality deteriorate in real world which leads towards feeling of loneliness which leads towards identity gap hence lack of social support it builds superficial identity (Jessica L. Rhodes 2014)

H0 3- There is significant difference between male and female in context of social media interaction

H0 4- Women, in comparison to men, scores high on social media addiction scale

At this aspect of analysis we found no such gender differences on the way of interaction on social media. As we do not find any kind of significant relationship based on social media users.

A study done by DongHee Kima, SooCheong (Shawn) Jangb (2017) found that relationships between narcissism and gender in the context of social media, online sharing behavior are only based on the way of presenting themselves which defines their interaction effect.

Therefore we can not say that women are more addicted towards social media than male. But when we see narcissistic tendencies we found that those who are high users of social media are not that much narcissistic because social media is affecting both the gender equally. Eg – social media increases narcissism. But contradict to that social media decreasing narcissism not decreasing because of cultural influences as compared to low users of social media. Narcissism is a personality trait driven by culture.

It can be two reasons

1) In collectivistic culture like India where male are more narcissistic than females and in Individualistic culture females are more narcissistic than male.

2) Haferkamp et al. (2012) found that men and women differ in their self-presentations on SNSs. Women tend to be more likely to use SNSs to compare themselves with others and search for information, while men are more likely to look at other people's profiles to find friends. A study done by DongHee Kima, SooCheong (Shawn) Jangb (2017) found that relationships between narcissism and gender in the context of social media, online sharing behavior are only based on the way of presenting themselves which defines their interaction effect. They found similar result

H0 5 - Male show higher narcissistic tendency in contrast to female.

Higher user data is not showing any gender based discrimination but there is in low user. A study done by Olga Paramboukis, Jason Skues, Lisa Wise(2016 Australia) and other study done by Cecilie Schou Andreassen, Stale Pallesen, Mark D. Griffiths(2016 Norway) where female are more narcissistic than male due to the influence of social media. Also supported that in Individualistic culture female are more or equal narcissistic to male.

Nima Ghorbani, P.J. Watson, Stephen W. Krauss, And Mark N. Bing, H. Kristl Davison(2004)Narcissism failed to correlate with individualist values, but displayed negative associations with collectivist values, and religious interest.

Country like India where society is made up of collectivistic society and patriarchy system, which makes India a special case. In my study data is not showing any sex based discrimination due to impact of social media.Clearly understands due to social media specially country like India either female are becoming more narcissistic or male are becoming low on narcissism. Or another reason can be that society is moving towards individualistic culture.

Chapter V
Discussion

CHAPTER-V
DISCUSSION AND INTERPRETATION

The aim of the study is to reveal a composite effect of social media, narcissism and self-identity. The preceding chapter presented the result of this study. The results show how social media, narcissism and self identity affect each other. The present chapter is to discuss the findings of the study.

H0 1 – Higher Social media users will show higher scores on narcissism.

Pearson correlations were used in this study to determine the relationship between Social Media and Narcissism with its different dimensions, Personal Identity, Relationship Identity, Social Identity, Collective Identity and Superficial Identity.

The first hypothesis states that Higher Social media users will show higher scores on narcissism, results indicated a significant positive correlation between social media and narcissism which depicts that excessive use of social media will lead to develop a higher narcissistic tendency.

Getting support from Qualitative analysis Verbatim like, ―easy to get famous", ―I love sharing my photos, videos, and doing live chatting with my fans, it gives me recognition all over the world".

We can not claim Social media as a neutral platform, it has a powerful effect in tapping into people's desire to see or shape themselves in their own terms. Higher urge of defining their own self and the competition that has occurred by the concept of social media, the meaning of endless elements has been changed. More examples can be defined with a good example which can be beauty in the current scenario. Because of this issue, the ratio in plastic surgeries and editing the photos has been increased a lot. More interestingly it can be understood by how people present themselves in a very effective and acceptable manner. This idea of behavior can be understood by the concept of "Self- Verification".

Self-verification theory proposes that people prefer to be seen as they see themselves, even if their self-views are negative (Swann 2012). Self-verification theory is based on the premise that individuals want to affirm and thus stabilize their firmly held self-views. This idea was first articulated by Prescott Lecky (1945) who proposed that chronic self-views give people a strong sense of coherence. Self-verification theory (Swann 1983) developed Lecky's idea that stable self-view organize people's efforts to maximize coherence. Supporting qualitative analysis theme and verbatim is-

Salience - "It definitely provide a platform to express yourself as an individual but also plays an important role in an individual's thoughts about oneself"

Withdrawal- "From my point of view it's a good platform for how to be popular on this media, which makes you more famous than you are. If you have special "things" which are required according to demand."

Self Absorption - For the reason given above, it clearly shows that people have a powerful desire to confirm themselves, thus consequently, it shows that individuals have strong craving to affirm. Article given by Michael D.Barnett and Kendall J. Sharp (2017) describes their results under study suggesting that self-absorption and narcissism share a component of pathological self-focused attention, and that a dysregulated status-seeking mechanism may be involved in narcissism.

There have been a number of conceptualizations of pathological self awareness (Raskin & Hall, 1979; Wink, 1991) and maladaptive self focused attention (McKenzie & Hoyle, 2008; Pincus et al., 2009). Narcissism may be conceptualized as a pathological form of self-focused attention (Raskin & Hall, 1979; Wink, 1991). This maladaptive self-focused attention is a characteristic that can be seen in both self-absorption and narcissism scales (McKenzie & Hoyle, 2008; Pincus et al., 2009). In this study, we sought to explore the links between the maladaptive self-focused attention found in self-absorption and narcissism.

Self Identity - ―It definitely provide a platform to express yourself as an individual but also plays an important role in an individual's thoughts about oneself"

Self verification biased/ confirmation bias – a study done by Abdallah Alsaad, Abdallah Taamneh, Mohamad Noor Al-Jedaiah (2018) they try to find out the connection between increased rate of racist, hate crimes and hateful behavior. This research focuses on the relationship between social media and confirmation bias. Confirmation bias predicts that human beings have an unconscious propensity to search for, favor, recall, and interpret information in a way that confirms their previous beliefs and hypotheses, while giving disproportionately less attention to alternative possibilities which leads to polarization in beliefs.

Classic research in the selective exposure paradigm (Lazarsfeld, Berelson, & Gaudet, 1944) has demonstrated that people tend to prefer information that is consistent with their preexisting attitudes (―confirmation bias;" Hart et al., 2009). As a potential explanation of attitude-consistent choices, many studies refer to cognitive dissonance theory (Festinger, 1957), which states that inconsistencies in one's beliefs arouse mental discomfort: large body of research (e.g., Kunda, 1990) has shown that people are often driven to preserve their self-concept or worldviews, which may happen consciously or unconsciously with the illusion of still being objective.

Due to social media they can easily observe others' recommendations and evaluations of the content that is specific selective exposure to information towards their pre-conceived notion.It also supports with the idea that in people's freedom of choice are resulting into the selection of content that is likely to strengthen their initial viewpoints but on other hand it's unlikely to enhance their knowledge (Iyengar &Hahn, 2009; Stroud, 2011). Selective exposure online has also supported the notion of attitude-consistent choices (e.g., Garrett, 2009a; Knobloch-Westerwick & Meng, 2009).

Notorious confirmation bias is the result of self absorption and self verification which make people satisfy their self view. It becomes more adverse in context to narcissism. Such kind of disoriented and selective content is making people more narcissistic, which results into bad decision making and motivating human right violation.

Human rights violation – there are two types of narcissism grandiose and vulnerable. A study done by rebecca l. Kauten, Christopher t. Barry (2015) tries to identify the relation between adolescent narcissism and with different indices of pro and anti social behaviour. Results identified that grandiose narcissism has a positive relation with pro-social behaviour and vulnerable narcissism has positive relation with anti-social behaviour. A study done by Anna Z.Czarna, Marcin Zajenkowski, Oliwia Machiantowicz & Kinga Szymaniak (2019). The significant relationships between both forms of narcissism with aggression, hostility, anger and poor emotional managing. (form might be different) Findings suggest that narcissism is positively related to social media platforms significantly moderated the results and tend to become more violent. A study done by Jessica L. McCain and W. Keith Campbell (2018)

It has been clearly mentioned that latest crimes which are related to social media misinformation and fake news no country is equipped to deal with such kind of crimes

A social media post on Prophet Muhammad led to violence in Karnataka's Bengaluru on Tuesday. Major violence broke out in DJ Halli area after the protesters alleged that Congress MLA R Akhanda Srinivas Murthy's kin had allegedly uploaded a derogatory post about Prophet Muhammad on his Facebook account. The Maharashtra state administration is still trying to come to terms with the shocking lynching on 1 July 2020 in Dhule district in northern Maharashtra, where a restive mob of 3,500-plus villagers gathered outside the gram panchayat office in Rainpada village, broke open the locks, and killed five agricultural labourers on the suspicion that they were ‗child-lifters'. There have been 14 incidents of mob lynching and vigilante justice—fuelled by rumours spread on social media—in Maharashtra alone in less than a month since 8 June.

In 2012, for instance, a rumour that spread like wildfire on social media had the north-eastern people in Bengaluru fleeing the city overnight. ―These were not just random rumours, these are targeted. For example, the messages circulated in Bengaluru targeted Hindi-speaking migrants," said Pranesh Prakash, fellow at the Centre for Internet and Society, a Bengaluru-based think tank.

This was done through the lens of the Expectation Confirmation Biasness. Social Media is providing a platform where every performance is posited to follow an Expectation Confirmation Theory framework, in which social media users are either satisfied or dissatisfied depending on their subjective evaluation of performance.

H0 2 - Excessive use of social media will create dissociated self identity

Whenever we talk about self identity, it means how any person is recognizing or knowing himself in terms of ground base reality. It also refers to a balanced state of identification in respect to personal, relationship, social and collective identity. For my study I have chosen one other orientation of identity is superficial identity. With this identity it will help to understand the user's perception towards their identity formation influenced by social media. Lots of studies done to identify whether there is any relationship between social media and self identity formation impacted by social media. A study done by Madison Ganda (2014) identifies a relationship between identity development within online and offline social networking sites. In which they identify that there is no significant relationship.

Self is a person's essential being which distinguishes them from others especially in terms of introspection or reflexive action whereas Identity orientations refer to the relative importance that individuals place on various identity attributes or characteristics when constructing their self-definitions (Cheek, 1989). When we describe self identity it means how any person is recognizing or knowing himself in terms of ground base reality. Because, these different self-identity aspects can impact social behaviors in various ways (Ellemers, Spears & Doosje, 2002). Depending on which self-identity aspect is triggered, it may cause different behaviours and characteristics to surface. In the present study we have considered five different identity characteristics representing different domains of a person's self identity.Now a days where everyone has exposure to social media and they use social media platforms to understand themselves better,which directly affects people's perception of themselves.

Results show that in different domains of self-identity there is a positive and significant relationship between social media, personal identity, social identity and superficial identity.

The kind of relationship showing in the result table depicts that as social media will increase personal identity will decrease.

The line between the real person (or the „offline" one) and her projection onto social networking sites (her „online" self) is becoming blurred.(S. Hongladarom) due to which personal Identity is framing into personal identity deception which has become an increasingly important issue in the social media environment, where identity is forming without non verbal cues or artificial non verbal cues. Michail Tsikerdekis and Sherali Zeadally in his study he called it identity deception.(superficial identity).

Superficial identity- Under this study I found a significant positive relationship between social media and superficial identity. Reasons were found that, when a person is inclined towards addictive use of social media then the user's self disclosure (Self-disclosure refers to the process of revealing personal, intimate information about oneself to others.) quality deteriorates in the real world which leads towards feelings of loneliness which leads towards identity gaps hence lack of social support builds superficial identity (Jessica L. Rhodes 2014.)

Qualitative analysis supports by the theme and verbatim

"it's easy to make yourself occupied rather focusing on useless and irrelevant stuffs"

"It helps me to forget my personal problems and other issues which I face throughout the day. In fact, it helps me to run away from the harsh realities and negative vibes in life."

Social identity - significant positive relationship between social media and social identity supports the idea that society and new society is using technology undoubtly for their betterment. All these sites claims to make world open and connected, it brings people more close together, it helps in building common understanding. It is helping people to build community, a meaningful systematic change are happening around the world

Qualitative analysis supports by the theme and verbatim like-

"social media has provide me to be in touch of all my friends",

"provide lots of news and information",

"helps us to connect with the people around us",

"i am social keeda"

The reason can be that society and new society is using technology undoubtly for their betterment. These social media tools actually created something very beneficial in the world. They are working to unite lost friends and families. All these sites claim to make the world open and connected, it brings people more close together, it helps in building common understanding. It is helping people to build community, and meaningful systematic changes are happening around the world (being local connect global), and this is what I found in my study by getting a significantly positive relationship between social media and social identity.

Looking towards the actual fact we can say that social media tools are being used for changing society fundamentally. Social media is being used for manipulating human behavior. Under this study I found significant positive relationship between social media and superficial identity reason were found was that, when person is inclined towards addictive use of social media then user's self disclosure quality deteriorate in real world which leads towards feeling of loneliness which leads towards identity gap hence lack of social support it builds superficial identity (Jessica L. Rhodes 2014)

H0 3- There is significant difference between male and female in context of social media interaction

H0 4- Women, in comparison to men, scores high on social media addiction scale

At this aspect of analysis we found no such gender differences on the way of interaction on social media. As we do not find any kind of significant relationship based on social media users.

A study done by DongHee Kima, SooCheong (Shawn) Jangb (2017) found that relationships between narcissism and gender in the context of social media, online sharing behavior are only based on the way of presenting themselves which defines their interaction effect.

Therefore we can not say that women are more addicted towards social media than male. But when we see narcissistic tendencies we found that those who are high users of social media are not that much narcissistic because social media is affecting both the gender equally. Eg – social media increases narcissism. But contradict to that social media decreasing narcissism not decreasing because of cultural influences as compared to low users of social media. Narcissism is a personality trait driven by culture.

It can be two reasons

1) In collectivistic culture like India where male are more narcissistic than females and in Individualistic culture females are more narcissistic than male.

2) Haferkamp et al. (2012) found that men and women differ in their self-presentations on SNSs. Women tend to be more likely to use SNSs to compare themselves with others and search for information, while men are more likely to look at other people's profiles to find friends. A study done by DongHee Kima, SooCheong (Shawn) Jangb (2017) found that relationships between narcissism and gender in the context of social media, online sharing behavior are only based on the way of presenting themselves which defines their interaction effect. They found similar result

H0 5 - Male show higher narcissistic tendency in contrast to female.

Higher user data is not showing any gender based discrimination but there is in low user. A study done by Olga Paramboukis, Jason Skues, Lisa Wise(2016 Australia) and other study done by Cecilie Schou Andreassen, Stale Pallesen, Mark D. Griffiths(2016 Norway) where female are more narcissistic than male due to the influence of social media. Also supported that in Individualistic culture female are more or equal narcissistic to male.

Nima Ghorbani, P.J. Watson, Stephen W. Krauss, And Mark N. Bing, H. Kristl Davison(2004)Narcissism failed to correlate with individualist values, but displayed negative associations with collectivist values, and religious interest.

Country like India where society is made up of collectivistic society and patriarchy system, which makes India a special case. In my study data is not showing any sex based discrimination due to impact of social media.Clearly understands due to social media specially country like India either female are becoming more narcissistic or male are becoming low on narcissism. Or another reason can be that society is moving towards individualistic culture.

CPSIA information can be obtained
at www.ICGtesting.com
Printed in the USA
BVHW071039130223
658295BV00015B/1825

9 784532 844721